Longman

Physics

11–14

Jennifer Clifford | Miles Hudson

Penny Johnson | Gary Philpott

Contents

Contents

Contents

Contents

How to use this book

Introduction: Each section starts with a question. The question should help you to think about what you are going to study. You should be able to answer this question by the time you finish the section.

Quick check questions occur throughout the section. These will help you and your teacher to check you have understood the section so far.

Fact boxes give you some interesting facts linked to the section.

Key words: Important scientific words are in bold the first time that they appear in a section. You will also find a glossary at the back of the book. The glossary has a definition of each of these words.

Electricity and magnetism   SECTION **5**

5.1 Static electricity

Why does some clothing crackle when you undress? What causes lightning? Electricity is all around us – static electricity can build up on many objects. It can also make your hair stand on end!

All substances are made up of atoms. An atom consists of **protons** (positively charged particles) and **neutrons** (which have no charge). These particles are in the central **nucleus**. **Electrons** have a negative charge and they orbit the central nucleus.

An atom is electrically neutral. This means that an atom has the same number of positive charges as negative charges. Only the electrons can be moved because they are on the outside of the atom.

When a plastic ruler is rubbed with a dry cloth it will pick up little pieces of paper. What has happened to the plastic ruler to allow it to do this? The ruler is made of atoms and each atom has the same number of electrons and protons in it. It is electrically neutral. When a cloth is rubbed against the ruler friction helps to move some of the electrons. If the electrons are moved from the ruler onto the cloth then the ruler will have fewer electrons. The ruler therefore has a positive charge. The cloth will have extra electrons and it will have an overall negative charge.

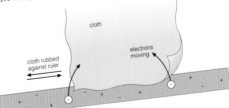

Figure 1.2 *The ruler is being charged up using the cloth.*

Sometimes the electrons will move from the cloth and onto the plastic, depending on the type of materials used. This will give the plastic a negative charge and the cloth a positive charge. Glass can also be charged up in this way. We call this type of charge **static electricity**. Any substance that will allow electricity to flow through it easily cannot be charged with static electricity and is called a **conductor**. The charge flows away and does not build up. Only an

1 What charge do each of the following have?
a) proton [1]
b) neutron [1]
c) electron [1]
[Total 3]

2 Why can't positive charges be rubbed off a material? [Total 2]

The ancient Greeks were the first people to notice the effects of static electricity. The amber beads they wore rubbed against their skin, became charged up, and soon became very dusty.

---

5 Electricity and magnetism

Summary

- A flow of current is the movement of electrica
- Electrons move from the negative terminal of
- Conventional current flow is from positive to
- In a series circuit the current flows round a cc
- In a parallel circuit the current splits into sepa
- A short circuit is a very easy route for the elec
- An insulator has a very high resistance to curr
- An ammeter measures current in amps and a v

Questions

1 Copy and complete the following sentences.

An electric current is a flow of _____. For this to happen there must be a complete _____. Current flows easily through a _____ but it does not flow easily through an _____. An _____ measures current and must be placed in _____ in a circuit. A voltmeter measures _____ and must be placed in _____ in a circuit.
[Total 4]

2 Match the symbols shown in Figure 2.9 to their names.
ammeter
voltmeter
wire
cell
bulb
switch [Total 4]

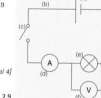

Figure 2.9

Summary boxes: Each sub section ends with a summary which will help you to draw together what you have just read. They will also help you revise.

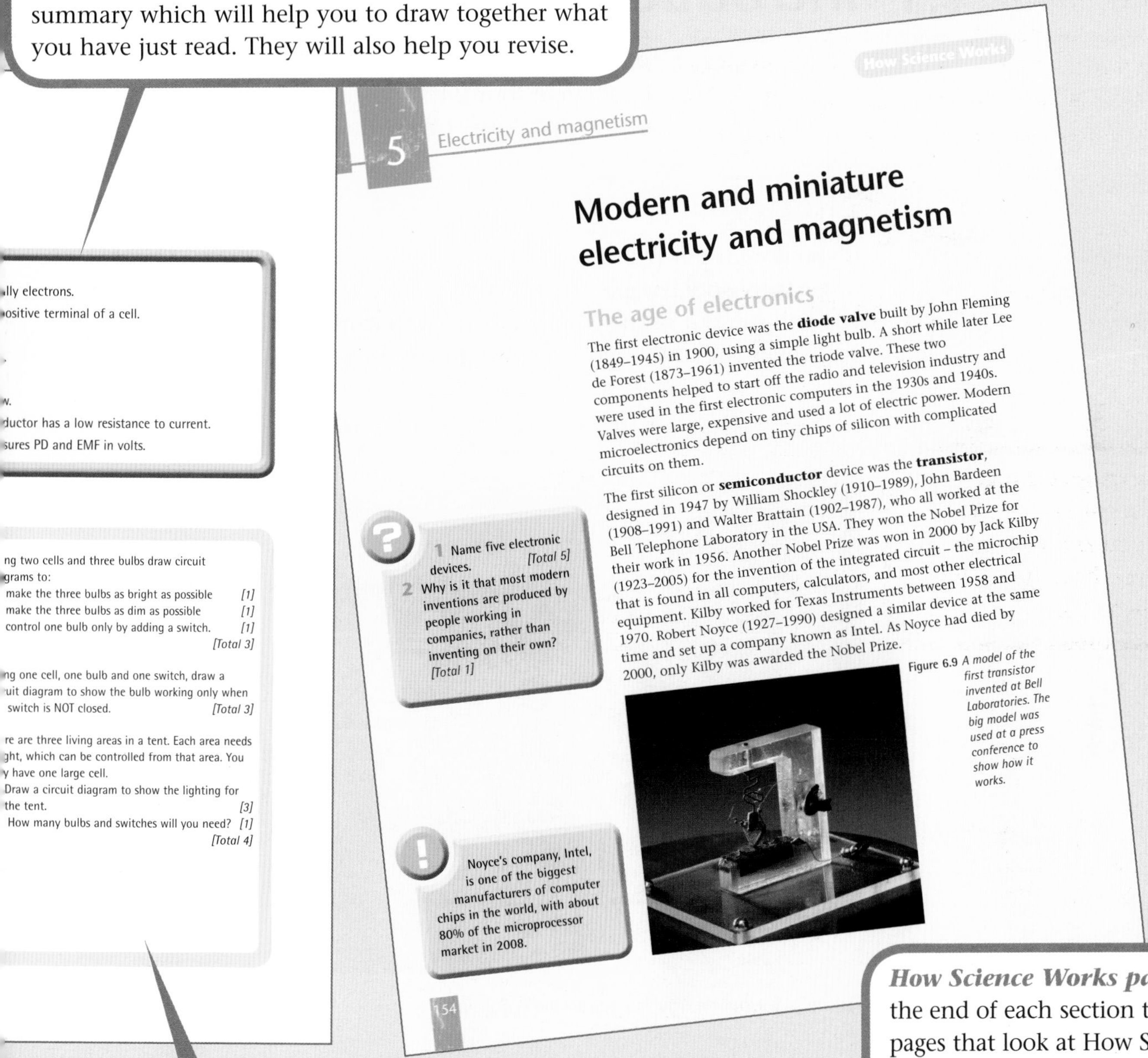

[partial text visible from adjacent page fragment]

lly electrons.
ositive terminal of a cell.

w.

ductor has a low resistance to current.
sures PD and EMF in volts.

ng two cells and three bulbs draw circuit
grams to:
make the three bulbs as bright as possible   *[1]*
make the three bulbs as dim as possible   *[1]*
control one bulb only by adding a switch.   *[1]*
  [Total 3]

ng one cell, one bulb and one switch, draw a
uit diagram to show the bulb working only when
switch is NOT closed.   *[Total 3]*

re are three living areas in a tent. Each area needs
ght, which can be controlled from that area. You
y have one large cell.
Draw a circuit diagram to show the lighting for
the tent.   *[3]*
How many bulbs and switches will you need? *[1]*
  [Total 4]

---

5 Electricity and magnetism

Modern and miniature electricity and magnetism

The age of electronics

The first electronic device was the **diode valve** built by John Fleming (1849–1945) in 1900, using a simple light bulb. A short while later Lee de Forest (1873–1961) invented the triode valve. These two components helped to start off the radio and television industry and were used in the first electronic computers in the 1930s and 1940s. Modern Valves were large, expensive and used a lot of electric power. Modern microelectronics depend on tiny chips of silicon with complicated circuits on them.

The first silicon or **semiconductor** device was the **transistor**, designed in 1947 by William Shockley (1910–1989), John Bardeen (1908–1991) and Walter Brattain (1902–1987), who all worked at the Bell Telephone Laboratory in the USA. They won the Nobel Prize for their work in 1956. Another Nobel Prize was won in 2000 by Jack Kilby (1923–2005) for the invention of the integrated circuit – the microchip that is found in all computers, calculators, and most other electrical equipment. Kilby worked for Texas Instruments between 1958 and 1970. Robert Noyce (1927–1990) designed a similar device at the same time and set up a company known as Intel. As Noyce had died by 2000, only Kilby was awarded the Nobel Prize.

?
1 Name five electronic devices.   *[Total 5]*
2 Why is it that most modern inventions are produced by people working in companies, rather than inventing on their own? *[Total 1]*

!
Noyce's company, Intel, is one of the biggest manufacturers of computer chips in the world, with about 80% of the microprocessor market in 2008.

Figure 6.9 *A model of the first transistor invented at Bell Laboratories. The big model was used at a press conference to show how it works.*

154

How Science Works pages: At the end of each section there are pages that look at How Science Works. Each topic on these pages is linked to part of the work in the section you have just read.

Question boxes: There are question boxes at the end of each sub section and each section. The questions towards the end of each box may be a little harder, to help you to see how well you have understood the work.

Some questions have an **R** next to them. These are research questions. You will need to use other books or the Internet to write a full answer to these questions.

In the end of section questions some questions have a **P** next to them. These questions can be used to help you plan practical investigations.

1.1 Introduction to energy

What is **energy?** Where do we get our energy from and what happens to it? Energy exists in different forms. It can be transferred (moved from one place to another). We make use of these transfers in everyday life.

Energy

If you do not put petrol in a car, the car does not have the energy that it needs to work. People are the same; if you do not eat then eventually you will run out of the energy you need to work, play, keep warm and stay alive. The unit of energy is the **joule** (J).

Energy is the ability to do work

Figure 1.1 *How energy is used in everyday life.*

Forms of energy

- Ways of transferring energy – thermal (heat), electrical, light, sound.
- Ways of storing energy – kinetic, chemical, potential, nuclear.

Energy can be transferred in different forms, as listed above. Radios, hairdryers and washing machines all require **electrical** energy to make them work. Bunsen burners, candles and bonfires all produce **thermal** energy, which is sometimes called **heat** energy.

Petrol stores **chemical** energy and is burnt inside a car's engine to make the car work. Food contains the chemical energy we use inside our bodies to enable us to move and keep warm.

Kinetic energy is the energy that an object stores because it is moving. It is sometimes called movement energy.

Potential energy is the stored energy an object has because of its position or shape. This potential energy can be transferred, usually as kinetic energy. There are two types of potential energy: **gravitational potential** energy and **elastic potential** energy.

A vase on a shelf has gravitational potential energy. If the vase is knocked off the shelf its potential energy is released and the vase moves downwards until it smashes on the floor below.

Figure 1.2

A stretched elastic band has elastic potential energy (or **strain** energy). When this energy is released the elastic band can be made to fly through the air. Springs also store elastic potential energy when they are squashed or stretched.

Energy transfers

The wax in a candle contains chemical energy. When the candle burns the chemical energy is transferred into thermal energy and light energy.

These energy transfers can be shown using an **energy flow diagram:**

chemical energy → heat energy + light energy

A guitar transfers kinetic energy into sound energy. Plucking a string makes it vibrate and the kinetic energy is transferred into sound energy.

kinetic energy → sound energy

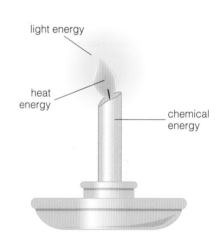

Figure 1.3 *Energy transfers in a burning candle.*

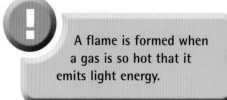

A flame is formed when a gas is so hot that it emits light energy.

Figure 1.4

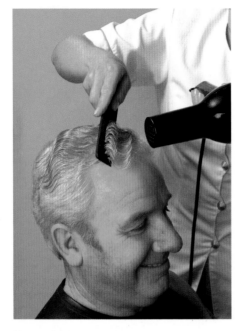

Figure 1.5

Hairdryers transfer electrical energy into thermal energy and kinetic energy. They also produce unwanted sound energy.

| electrical energy | → | heat energy | + | kinetic energy | + | sound energy |

Water stored behind a dam has gravitational potential energy. When the water is released, it flows downwards and gains kinetic energy. This energy can then be transferred to electrical energy in a **hydroelectric** power station.

| potential energy | → | kinetic energy | → | electrical energy |

A child on a swing is continually transferring kinetic energy into gravitational potential energy and back into kinetic energy as the child swings up and down. Eventually the swing stops as friction converts kinetic energy into thermal energy.

| potential energy | → | kinetic energy | → | thermal energy |

Conservation of energy

When energy is transferred, all the energy is transferred into other forms of energy. The law of conservation of energy states:

> Energy cannot be created or destroyed. It can only be transferred from one form to another.

Not all the forms of energy are useful. If the useful light energy and wasted thermal energy produced by a light bulb were measured and added together they would equal the amount of electrical energy supplied to the bulb.

> electrical energy in = thermal energy out + light energy out

? 1 Draw an energy flow diagram to show the energy transfers in Figure 1.2. Include what happens when the vase hits the ground. *[Total 4]*

Example
For every 100 J of electrical energy supplied to a lamp, 5 J is transferred as useful light energy and 95 J is transferred as unwanted thermal energy.

This can be shown using a **Sankey diagram** as shown in Figure 1.6. This shows that the lamp is only 5% efficient at doing the job it is designed to do.

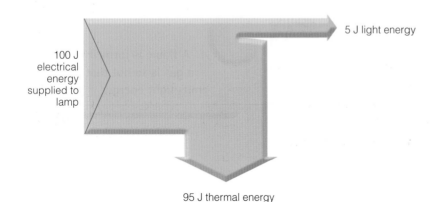

Figure 1.6 *Sankey diagram for a light bulb.*

The **efficiency** of a machine is the percentage of the energy that it transfers as useful energy.

$$\text{efficiency} = \frac{\text{useful energy transferred}}{\text{total energy transferred}} \times 100\%$$

Energy-saving lamps are about 25% efficient. For every 100 J of electrical energy supplied to them, they produce 25 J of light energy.

Figure 1.8 shows the overall energy transfers in a modern coal-fired power station.

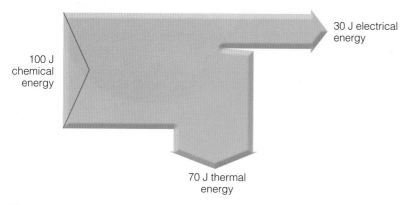

Figure 1.8 *Sankey diagram for a coal-fired power station.*

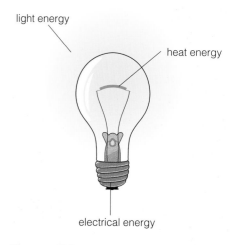

Figure 1.7 *Energy transfers in a lamp.*

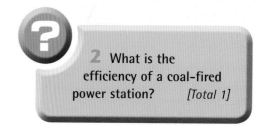

2 What is the efficiency of a coal-fired power station? *[Total 1]*

Energy from the Sun

The Earth would be a very cold planet without the Sun shining on it. The Sun radiates heat and light energy into space and a small fraction of this energy falls onto the Earth. Most of the Earth's energy is provided by the Sun. Without sunlight plants would not grow and animals would not survive.

Where does the energy go?

When the inside of a house is hotter than the outside, thermal energy escapes to the surroundings. Unless the heating system is kept switched on, the house will lose its thermal energy and cool down. Light energy and sound energy will also be lost. This is because light and sound are absorbed by materials inside the house and transferred to thermal energy.

Figure 1.9

The Earth is continually absorbing energy from the Sun but it is also losing energy into space.

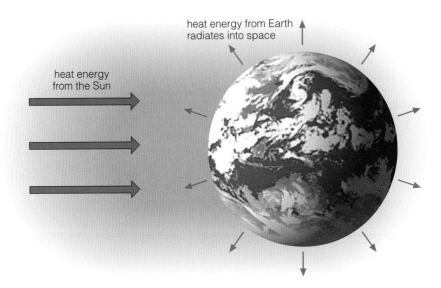

Figure 1.10

Most energy forms are eventually transferred into thermal energy. This thermal energy then radiates out into space. Kinetic energy is often transferred to thermal energy by friction. Substances often absorb other forms of energy and they get hotter as the energy is transferred to their molecules. The extra energy makes the molecules vibrate faster.

Summary

- Energy is the ability to do work.
- The unit of energy is the joule (J).
- Energy exists in different forms – heat, light, sound, electrical, etc.
- Energy cannot be created or destroyed, it can only be transferred from one form to another.
- Most of the Earth's energy comes from the Sun.

Questions

1 Copy and complete the following sentences.
Energy is the ability to do _____. Energy
cannot be _____ or _____, it
can only be transferred from one form to
_____.
[Total 4]

2 Which two of the following are units of energy?
newton   joule   Celsius   kilogram   kilojoule
[Total 2]

3 What forms of energy are transferred by the
following:
a) a burning candle   [2]
b) a violin   [2]
c) an electric toaster   [2]
d) a petrol engine?   [2]
[Total 8]

4 Match the two halves of the sentences together.
Write out the correct complete sentence.

a) A lamp transfers...   chemical energy
                                to heat, light,
                                sound and kinetic
                                energy.   [1]
b) A radio transfers...   gravitational
                                potential energy
                                to kinetic energy.
                                                  [1]
c Exploding dynamite   electrical energy
   transfers...   to thermal energy
                                and light energy.
                                                  [1]
d) A falling apple transfers... electrical energy
                                to sound energy.
                                                  [1]
[Total 4]

5 Look at Figure 1.1 on page 2. List the energy
transfers you can see taking place.   [Total 6]

6 Draw energy flow diagrams for the following devices:
a) a candle   [3]
b) an electric bell   [3]
c) a drum kit   [2]
d) an electric kettle   [2]
e) a petrol driven lawnmower   [4]
f) a nuclear power station.   [4]
[Total 18]

7 This toy bounces up and down on a spring.

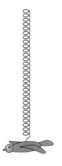

potential energy ⇄ kinetic energy

a) Explain why there are two arrows between the
boxes in the energy flow diagram.   [1]
b) The toy will eventually stop. Explain why this
will happen in terms of energy transfers.   [3]
c) i) What are the two forms of potential energy?
   ii) At which part of each bounce does the toy
       have these forms?   [4]
[Total 8]

8 For every 100 J of energy contained in petrol used by
a car it will transfer 25 J of this energy into kinetic
energy. The remaining energy is wasted as heat.
a) Draw a Sankey diagram to show the energy
transfers involved.   [5]
b) How efficient is the car? Explain your answer. [2]
[Total 7]

1.2 Thermal energy

Are heat and temperature the same thing? How does thermal energy flow through solids, liquids and gases? Heat flows through everything. However, some substances are better than others at transferring heat.

Thermal energy and temperature

Temperature is measured in degrees Celsius (°C) and indicates how hot something is. Heat is a form of energy and is measured in joules (J).

The hotter an object is, the more thermal energy it contains, but heat and temperature are not the same thing.

Heating a beaker of water

Heating a small mass of water from room temperature to boiling point will require a certain amount of thermal energy. If twice the mass of water is heated then twice as much thermal energy is required to raise the temperature of the water by the same amount. The same thing happens when using a kettle to boil water to make cups of tea. Each cup of tea will be at the same temperature but the more cups you make, the more thermal energy you need.

Heating different substances

The atoms that make up any substance move randomly. Heating the substance will make the atoms move faster, increasing the **internal energy** of the substance and causing its temperature to rise.

To heat 1 kg of copper from 20 °C to 21 °C requires 390 J of thermal energy. To raise the temperature of 1 kg of aluminium by the same amount requires 910 J of thermal energy. The amount of thermal energy required to raise 1 kg of a substance by 1 °C is called the **specific heat capacity** of the substance.

Heat transfer by conduction

Thermal energy travels from hot regions to cold regions. If you hold an iron bar in a fire, thermal energy will travel along the bar to your hand and could be rather painful.

Figure 2.1 *Heating water using electrical energy.*

> **!** It requires 4.2 J of energy to raise the temperature of 1 g of water by 1°C. This amount of energy is called a calorie.

> **?** 1 How much energy is needed to;
> a) heat 1 kg of copper from 40°C to 45°C? [1]
> b) heat 2 kg of aluminium from 30°C to 31°C [1]
> [Total 2]

Conductors and insulators

Solids which heat travels through quickly are called good **thermal conductors**. Materials that do not let heat flow through them very well are called **insulators**.

When cooking food in a frying pan we want the heat to pass through the bottom of the pan to the food. Therefore the bottom of the pan is made from a good conductor. We do not want the heat to pass through the handle and burn our hand. The handle is made from a good insulator such as wood or plastic.

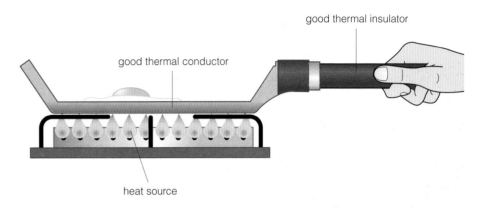

Figure 2.2 *A frying pan is a combination of a good conductor and a good insulator.*

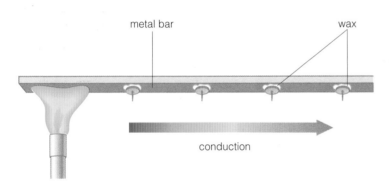

Figure 2.3 *Thermal conduction can be shown by attaching drawing pins to a metal bar with wax. As the heat travels along the bar, the wax melts and the drawing pins fall off one by one.*

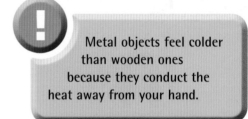

Metal objects feel colder than wooden ones because they conduct the heat away from your hand.

Drinks mats are made from good insulating materials to reduce the rate at which heat is conducted from a hot cup to the surface of a table. Hot water pipes are lagged with foam to reduce heat losses from the pipe.

Keeping warm

When people go outside on a cold day, they wear more clothes than they would on a hot day. The clothes act as an insulator and reduce the rate at which heat is lost to the surroundings. Mountaineers and skiers wear lots of thin layers of clothing rather than one thick layer. Air is then trapped between the layers, keeping the person warmer because trapped air is a good insulator.

Figure 2.4 *A mountaineer wears clothes with good insulating properties.*

Particle theory of conduction

When a solid material is heated its particles vibrate faster. When the particles are vibrating they collide with neighbouring particles. This causes the neighbouring particles to vibrate faster as well. The thermal energy is passed along the chain of particles from one end of the material to the other. This process is called **thermal conduction**.

Metals are good thermal conductors because the energy is also passed on by fast-moving electrons. The electrons are free to move from place to place and they quickly transfer their thermal energy to other electrons and atoms. Liquids are poor conductors because thermal energy is not easily transferred from one particle to another. The particles in a gas are a long way apart and therefore gases are not good conductors of heat. In a vacuum there are no particles, therefore thermal energy cannot be transferred by thermal conduction.

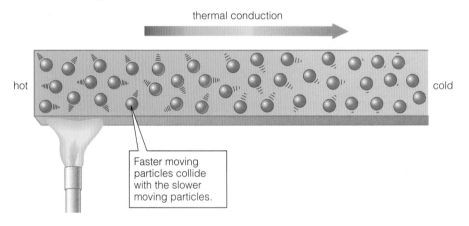

Figure 2.5 *Particle model of heat conduction.*

Heat transfer by convection

Hot fluids rise and transfer thermal energy from one place to another. This process is called **convection**.

The hot air above a burning candle rises and colder air flows in from the sides to replace it. This movement of air is known as a **convection current**. When air is heated, it expands. The same mass of air now occupies a larger volume, making it less dense than the colder air around it. As the warmer air has a lower density, it moves upwards in the same way that bubbles of gas rise to the top of a fizzy drink.

Convection is also the main method of heat transfer in liquids. In both liquids and gases the particles are free to move and flow from one region to another. Convection cannot take place in solids because the particles are bonded together, preventing them from flowing.

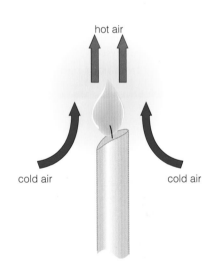

Figure 2.6 *Convection current round a burning candle.*

2 Give two reasons why copper is a good thermal conductor. *[Total 4]*

3 Sketch an ice lolly, and show the convection currents in the air near it. *[Total 1]*

Convection in the home

Convection currents are very useful for heating rooms. A heater on one side of a room will warm up the air around it. The warm air rises and creates a convection current that transfers thermal energy from one side of the room to the other.

Convection currents are also responsible for cold draughts that can blow across the floor in poorly insulated houses.

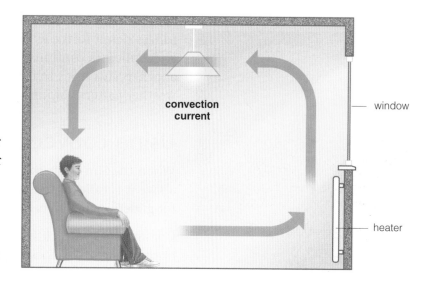

Figure 2.7 *Convection current around a room.*

Coastal breezes

Convection also causes breezes on the coast on warm days. During the day the land is heated by the Sun more quickly than the sea. This happens because the heat capacity of the water is larger than the heat capacity of the land. Convection causes the air above the land to rise. Cold air blows in from the sea to replace the air that has risen, causing an onshore breeze. At night this is reversed. The land cools more quickly than the sea and convection currents create an offshore breeze.

Figure 2.8 *Coastal breezes caused by convection during the day and at night.*

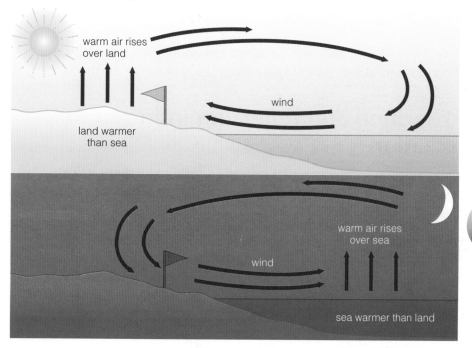

Most sailing boats and windsurfers will sail back to shore before the Sun sets so that they are not forced to sail against an offshore wind.

Windy weather

Temperatures around the world vary enormously, from the very hot Sahara desert to the extremely cold polar regions. The Earth's atmosphere is continually being heated in one region and cooled in another. This leads to large scale convection currents that contribute to weather patterns around the world.

Using convection currents to fly

When the Sun heats the land during the day the hot air that rises above it is called a **thermal**. Thermals can be used to provide the lift for gliders, paragliders and hang gliders.

Coastal areas with cliffs are good for paragliding because when the onshore breeze reaches the cliff, it rises rapidly. This creates a strong upward airflow that provides excellent lift for the paraglider.

Hot air balloons also use convection to keep them in the air. Gas burners underneath the balloon heat the air inside making it less dense than the colder air outside the balloon. If the air inside the balloon is not kept hot, it cools down and the balloon slowly loses height. To come down more quickly the pilot pulls on a rope to release hot air from the top of the balloon.

Figure 2.9 *Making use of convection currents.*

Heat transfer by radiation

Heat is transferred by **radiation** when it travels as an electromagnetic wave, i.e as visible light and infra-red radiation. This is how thermal energy travels across empty space from the Sun to the Earth.

Absorbing and reflecting infra-red radiation

Silver surfaces are very good at reflecting infra-red radiation. This means when the Sun shines on an object that has a silvered surface, most of the heat is reflected and very little is absorbed.

White surfaces are also poor absorbers of radiation. Houses in hot countries are often painted white so that they reflect most of the infra-red radiation during the day, keeping the house cooler inside. Black surfaces are good absorbers of infra-red radiation. Wearing black clothes on a hot sunny day means that you absorb radiation more quickly than if you wear white clothes. This is why many people in hot countries wear white clothing, particularly if they spend a lot of time out in the sun.

Figure 2.10 *White houses in a hot climate.*

Emitting infra-red radiation

When an object is hotter it emits more infra-red radiation from its surfaces. A black object is much better at emitting radiation than a silver object. Saucepans and metal kettles often have shiny outside surfaces to reduce heat losses by radiation. Central heating radiators are usually painted white but they radiate heat better when they are painted black.

Heat transfer by evaporation

A puddle on the pavement will disappear even though the temperature of the water has not reached boiling point, 100 °C. When liquid water turns into water vapour, it is called **evaporation**. When a beaker of water is heated to boiling point, water throughout the beaker turns into gas and bubbles of steam rise through the liquid water. If the water in a beaker is at a temperature lower than 100 °C, it does not boil but water will still evaporate from the surface, until eventually there is no water left in the beaker.

Evaporation is a surface effect, whereas boiling occurs throughout the liquid.

Particle explanation of evaporation

Particles in a liquid are close together and move around randomly. Some particles will be moving faster than others. When fast-moving particles reach the surface they escape from the liquid and form a vapour. Some of these particles travel back into the liquid but others escape completely. In this way the liquid slowly loses particles to the surroundings and the liquid evaporates.

Heating the liquid increases the average speed of the particles and means that more particles are likely to escape. Therefore the rate of evaporation increases.

The higher energy particles are the ones most likely to escape, leaving behind the slower-moving particles. As the particles with the higher energy have escaped, the temperature of the liquid decreases.

Wet skin on a windy day

When your body is wet or you are wearing wet clothes, your body heats this water. Thermal energy from your body is being transferred to the water, making the water molecules evaporate faster. In this way

Figure 2.11 *A black coffee pot will emit more infra-red radiation than a silver one.*

! Central heating radiators transfer the majority of the heat to a room by convection and not by radiation. Air close to the radiator is heated and this creates convection currents.

? 4 Sam says 'You can see bubbles of air in the liquid when water is boiling, but when a puddle is evaporating the bubbles are too small to see.' Explain what is wrong with this statement (there is more than one thing!).

[Total 2]

thermal energy is being transferred from your body to the surroundings, making you feel cold.

Drying yourself with a towel when you first get out of a bath or swimming pool reduces the amount of water on your skin and therefore you lose less heat by evaporation.

If the wind is blowing you lose more heat from your body and you feel colder. This happens in the same way as when a saucer of water evaporates. On a windy day the molecules are more likely to escape completely from the liquid because they are swept away by the wind blowing over its surface.

You can demonstrate this effect by dabbing a drop of water onto the back of your hand and then blowing across it.

Figure 2.12

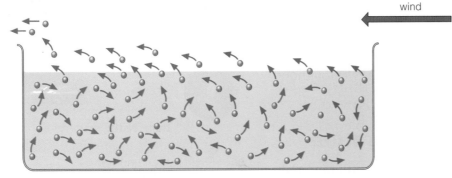

Figure 2.13 *Wind blowing molecules away from the surface of a liquid.*

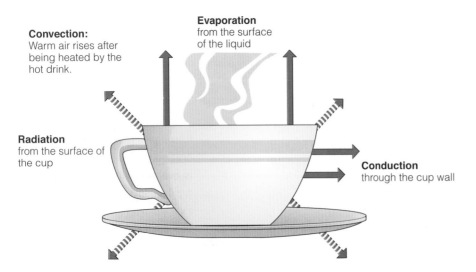

Figure 2.14 *Heat losses from a hot drink.*

Reducing heat losses

Keeping a drink hot

A hot cup of tea or coffee will lose thermal energy by the four methods of heat transfer: conduction, convection, radiation and evaporation.

To keep the drink hot for a long time each of these heat transfer methods needs to be reduced.

Packaging for take-away drinks can be very effective at keeping the drink hot. The cup may be made from a poor conductor such as polystyrene. This reduces heat conduction and also makes the cup easier to hold because the outer surface is not so hot. A plastic lid prevents air above the liquid transferring heat away by convection and also reduces heat loss by evaporation. Polystyrene cups are usually white and therefore they are not good thermal radiators.

Trapping air

Many insulating materials contain trapped air. Like other gases, air is a poor thermal conductor. To be a good insulator the air needs to be trapped, otherwise the air will transfer thermal energy by convection. Woollen jumpers help people keep warm because air is trapped between the fibres. Many of the fabrics used in modern outdoor clothing use trapped air to help reduce heat loss by conduction.

Animals have feathers or fur to trap the air and insulate them from the cold. For example, a polar bear has thick fur (Figure 2.15).

Your body also uses trapped air to help keep you warm on a cold day. When you are cold the tiny hairs on your skin stand up and trap air between them.

Reducing thermal energy losses from the home

In colder countries keeping a house warm can use a lot of energy. Not only is this very expensive, it is it is also a waste of the world's valuable energy resources. Most electricity is generated by burning fossil fuels in power stations. The carbon dioxide produced when fossil fuels burn is contributing to global warming. Using less electricity for lighting, televisions, computers and other electrical appliances can also save a lot of energy in the home.

Figure 2.15

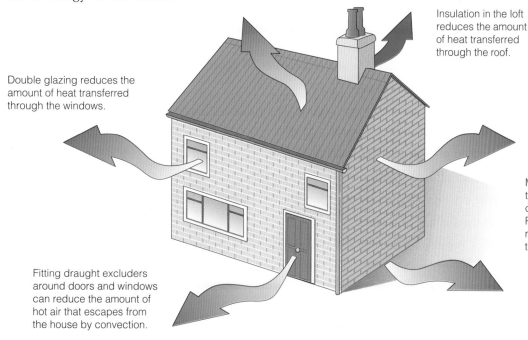

Insulation in the loft reduces the amount of heat transferred through the roof.

Double glazing reduces the amount of heat transferred through the windows.

Most houses are made from two layers of brick, with a cavity (gap) between them. Putting insulation in the cavity reduces the heat transferred through the walls.

Fitting draught excluders around doors and windows can reduce the amount of hot air that escapes from the house by convection.

Figure 2.16 *Reducing energy losses from an existing house.*

north-facing roof covered in earth and plants

wooden walls

earth bank on north side

small, double-glazed windows

conservatory on south side of house absorbs heat from the Sun

Figure 2.17 *A modern 'ecohouse' (the INTEGER house at Watford).*

5 Explain how the features of the INTEGER house reduce the amount of energy needed for heating   *[Total 4]*

Summary

- Temperature is a measure of how hot an object is and is measured in degrees Celsius (°C).
- Heat is a form of energy and is measured in joules (J).
- Thermal energy is transferred by four main methods – conduction, convection, radiation and evaporation.
- Conduction is the main method of heat transfer in solids.
- Convection is the main method of heat transfer in liquids and gases.
- Thermal energy can transfer across a vacuum by radiation but not by conduction and convection.
- Evaporation takes place at the surface of a liquid.
- Insulators are used to reduce the rate of thermal energy transfer.

Questions

1 Heat can be transferred by conduction, _____, radiation and _____. A good thermal _____ is a substance through which _____ travels quickly. An _____ does not let heat flow through it well. When heat is transferred by convection, _____ _____ rise. Thermal energy travels from the Sun to the Earth by _____. Wet skin will dry quicker by evaporation on a _____, _____ day. *[Total 5]*

2 Which one of the following statements best describes:
  a) conduction *[1]*
  b) convection *[1]*
  c) radiation *[1]*
  d) evaporation? *[1]*
  i) The transfer of thermal energy by electromagnetic waves that can pass through empty space.
  ii) Collisions between molecules transfer energy through solid materials.
  iii) Higher energy molecules escape from the surface of a liquid.
  iv) Hot fluids rise through the cooler and denser fluid surrounding them. *[Total 4]*

3 Sort the following materials into good thermal conductors and good thermal insulators.
  feathers   copper   aluminium   polythene
  iron   tin   fur   wood *[Total 8]*

4 In hot countries, the air conditioning units are often positioned close to the ceiling. Why is this? *[Total 3]*

5 a) Which heat transfer method is responsible for cold draughts in poorly insulated houses? *[1]*
  b) How can these cold draughts be prevented? *[3]*
  [Total 4]

6 The table below shows the insulation costs and annual energy bill savings for a three bedroom semi-detached house built in the 1930s.

Insulation method	Cost of installation (£)	Saving each year (£)
Fitting double glazing	4000	450
Fitting loft insulation	140	120
Injecting cavity wall insulation	500	100
Fitting jacket to hot water tank	10	30

  a) Draw two bar charts to display the cost of insulation and the annual saving for each method of insulation. *[8]*
  b) Which method saves the most money each year? *[1]*
  c) Which energy saving method costs most to fit? *[1]*
  d) How long will it take for double glazing to pay for itself? *[1]*
  e) Which method has the shortest payback time? *[1]*
  [Total 12]

7 Explain the difference between heat and temperature. *[Total 4]*

8 250 ml of water is heated from 20°C to 100°C to make a cup of tea. This requires 84 kJ of thermal energy.
  a) To what temperature would 42 kJ of energy heat the 250 ml of water? *[2]*
  b) How much thermal energy would be required to make four mugs of tea? *[3]*
  c) If 25% of the thermal energy produced by the kettle is lost to the surroundings, how much electrical energy will be transferred to heat energy when making four mugs of tea? *[4]*
  [Total 9]

1.3 Energy resources

Where will we get our energy from in one hundred years time? Which energy resources rely upon the Sun? Most of our energy comes from fossil fuels. These will run out and we will have to use other sources of energy. Burning fossil fuels also contributes to global warming because of the carbon dioxide produced.

Renewable and non-renewable energy resources

Many of the world's energy resources are not replaceable. These are called **non-renewable** energy resources. Fossil fuels such as coal and oil are good examples of non-renewable energy resources. They have taken millions of years to form and there is a limited supply that will eventually run out.

Other energy resources will not run out. These are called **renewable** energy resources. Solar energy is continuously reaching the Earth from the Sun. No matter how much of this solar energy is used one day, it will be replaced by more the next day, until the Sun eventually dies in about 6 billion years time.

Renewable	Non-renewable
solar	coal
wave	gas
tidal	oil
wind	nuclear
hydroelectric	
geothermal	
biomass	

Table 3.1 *Renewable and non-renewable energy resources.*

The difference between renewable energy resources and non-renewable energy resources is therefore the time it takes for them to be replaced. Non-renewable resources like fossil fuels would take millions of years to be replaced. Renewable energy resources are replaced in a relatively short period of time.

Generating electricity is the main use for most of these energy resources. Therefore to make the world's non-renewable energy resources last longer we need to use more renewable energy resources and use electricity more efficiently.

Fossil fuels

Coal, oil and natural gas are all **fossil fuels**. They have been formed over millions of years from the fossilised remains of trees, plants and sea creatures. The formation of fossil fuels is indirectly dependent on the Sun because the plants and animals could not have lived without the Sun's energy.

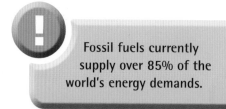

Coal can be burnt on open fires and in central heating boilers to heat people's homes directly. However most of the coal mined in the United Kingdom is burnt at power stations to generate electricity. The two main disadvantages of using coal to generate electricity are that when it burns it produces carbon dioxide and sulphur dioxide. Sulphur dioxide emissions can produce acid rain. Carbon dioxide emissions contribute to the **greenhouse effect** that is thought to be responsible for **global warming**.

Natural gas is used for heating in homes and factories. Natural gas is mostly made of methane gas but it does contain other gases such as ethane and propane. Natural gas is also burnt in power stations to generate electricity and, like coal, produces carbon dioxide.

Crude oil is refined to make many different products, including petrol and diesel for use in cars, buses and lorries. Petrol and diesel produce carbon dioxide when they burn, and also produce other polluting chemicals. It is much more difficult to find renewable resources for use in transport than it is to replace fossil fuels in power stations.

> **!** Fossil fuels currently supply over 85% of the world's energy demands.

Figure 3.1 *Coal-fired power station.*

Nuclear energy

Nuclear **fission** is used in power stations to generate electricity. Uranium-235 is the fuel that is used. A uranium atom breaks up and releases energy when a relatively slow moving **neutron** hits it. The atom also releases more neutrons. These hit other uranium atoms that also break up. This is called a **chain reaction**.

The power station would explode if this reaction were allowed to take place too quickly. To control the reaction boron rods are used. The boron absorbs some of the neutrons released in the reaction. If the boron rods are lowered into the reactor, there are fewer neutrons available to cause fission and the reaction slows down. To speed the reaction up, the boron rods are raised.

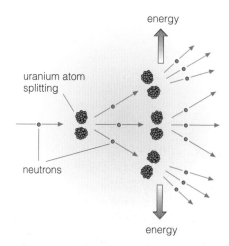

Figure 3.2 *Nuclear fission chain reaction.*

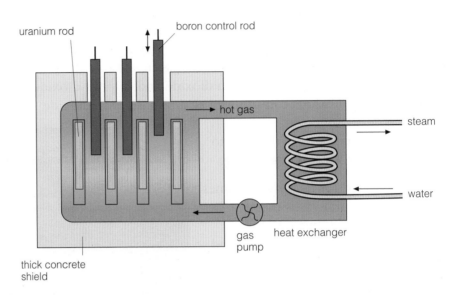

Figure 3.3 *A nuclear reactor.*

Some of the advantages of nuclear power are:

- a lot of energy is released from a small mass of uranium.
- supplies of uranium will last for a long time.
- nuclear fission does not release carbon dioxide.

However, some people are concerned about nuclear power because:

- a nuclear accident can cause a major international disaster.
- the waste produced stays radioactive for thousands of years.
- nuclear energy technology can also be used to make nuclear weapons.

1 Nuclear power does not contribute to global warming. Why is this?

[Total 1]

Solar energy

Solar energy comes directly from the Sun. Light and infra-red radiation travel across space as electromagnetic waves. Without solar energy life on Earth could not exist. Green plants are well adapted to capture this energy and store it as chemical energy in their leaves.

For solar energy to supply a significant proportion of the world's energy requirements, it will need to be converted into other useful forms of energy on a large scale.

Photocells like those used to power satellites and to power calculators, convert light energy directly into electrical energy. Photocells are relatively expensive and a lot of them are needed to produce quite small amounts of electricity.

In the Mojave Desert in southern California, 600 000 computer controlled curved mirrors are used to produce steam for generating electricity.

In hot countries solar energy is used to heat water directly. Water is pumped through **solar panels** on the roof of the building. The water is heated by the sunlight and then stored in a hot water tank. The main problem is that the water cannot be heated at night. Once the tank of hot water has been used, it cannot be replaced using solar energy until the next day.

Figure 3.4 *Solar cells to generate electricity.*

Wind energy

When the wind blows it is a valuable energy resource, driving wind turbines that generate electricity. To generate sufficient amounts of electricity, wind turbines are grouped together on wind farms. These wind farms need to be in a place where there are often strong winds. Suitable sites are often on the coast or in hilly regions.

Figure 3.5 *A wind farm in Wales.*

Electrical wind generators do produce low level noise pollution but the main problem is that they can spoil the appearance of scenic areas and some people think that they kill birds.

Wave energy

Waves at sea are caused by the wind stirring up the surface of the water. Wave energy can be captured and used to generate electricity. This can also be done by a generator built into a cliff, or by generators floating on the sea (see Figure 4.5 on page 29).

Just as with wind energy, we cannot rely on there being sufficient energy available when it is needed. To generate enough energy, a large area of sea needs to be used in a location that frequently has large waves.

? 2 Why are solar panels more common in countries like Greece and Spain than in the UK?

[Total 1]

! Windmills originated in Persia around 640 BC. They were not used in Europe until the 11th century AD.

? 3 Why can't we just use wind turbines to generate our electricity?

[Total 2]

Tidal energy

As the Earth rotates, the Moon's gravitational field causes the world's oceans to rise and fall twice a day. The best places for capturing this **tidal energy** are in large river estuaries where the water can be used to drive turbines as it flows out of the estuary after a high tide. Although the heights of tides do vary they are still very reliable: high and low tides will always occur twice a day.

Finding suitable locations can be difficult. A barrage needs to be built across the estuary to hold the water in place before releasing it through turbines in a controlled manner. These barrages form an obstruction to the movement of boats and fish. The large area of water trapped above the barrage causes flooding and changes the habitat of the wildlife there.

Figure 3.6 *Tidal-stream turbines can also be placed where the tides cause strong currents to flow.*

Hydroelectric energy

Figure 3.7 shows the energy transfers in a hydroelectric power station. Water flowing in rivers can be used to generate electricity. Usually a dam needs to be built across a valley to save the water until it is needed. Hydroelectricity can only be used where there is a good rainfall.

As with tidal energy, the large area of water trapped behind the dam causes flooding and changes the habitat of wildlife. In addition some houses may be flooded and the people will have to move.

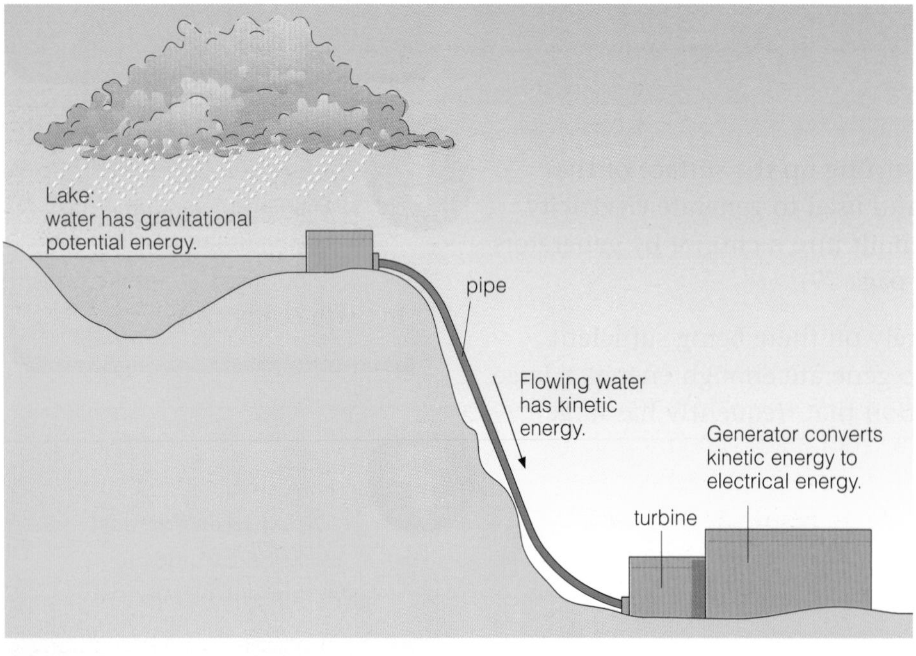

Geothermal energy

The eruption of a volcano gives an indication of how much thermal energy there is underneath the Earth's crust. In places such as Iceland, which is close to a gap between the Earth's tectonic plates, geysers may release this energy less violently.

At 5 km below the Earth's surface the rocks are at a temperature of about 185 °C. Cold water can be pumped down through these hot rocks to produce hot water. The

Lake: water has gravitational potential energy.

pipe

Flowing water has kinetic energy.

Generator converts kinetic energy to electrical energy.

turbine

Figure 3.7 *A hydroelectric power station.*

hot water can be used for local heating systems or to make steam that can be used to generate electricity.

Geothermal energy is available continuously. It will not run out while humans are living on the Earth although local areas of hot rocks may cool down and become unusable. It is therefore a renewable energy resource. It does not depend upon the Sun as its original source of energy.

Biomass

Biomass refers to the chemical energy stored in plant and vegetable matter. Sewage, dung, rotting food and vegetable matter can be fermented to produce methane gas that can then be burnt. Methane gas produced this way is called **biogas**. Fermentation can also be used to produce alcohol from sugar cane. In Brazil the alcohol is mixed with petrol to power cars that have been adapted to use this fuel.

In locations where other energy resources are not available animal dung is collected and dried. The dried dung is then made into cakes that are burnt to cook food or to provide heating at night.

Wood is also a form of biomass that can be used to generate electricity. Once a tree is chopped down it can take a very long time for a new one to grow. Wood was therefore previously regarded as a non-renewable energy resource. Wood from managed forests is a renewable energy resource. In a managed forest, when the trees in one area of a forest are cut down, new ones are planted straight away. By controlling how many trees are cut down each year, the new trees have time to grow sufficiently before that area of the forest needs to be used again. However it would need a lot of land to grow enough biomass to meet our energy needs.

Reducing the use of electrical energy

Electrical energy is a very convenient way of transferring energy. Electricity is not an energy resource, as it is generated using other forms of energy. It can be easily supplied to where it is needed and can be transferred into other useful forms of energy. As more countries become more developed, and people have higher living standards, the demand for electricity grows. Reducing the use of electrical energy will make a significant contribution to conserving the world's energy resources and also help reduce the emission of greenhouse gases.

Figure 3.8 *A geyser in Iceland.*

! Geothermal energy is used in over 20 countries around the world to generate electricity and to provide hot water for homes.

! The first cow dung fuelled power station was built in the UK at Holsworthy, Devon.

? 4 Write down four different ways in which biomass can be used as an energy resource.

[Total 4]

Ways of saving electrical energy at home

We can use less electricity at home by:

- switching off electrical equipment when it is not in use (remember that appliances are still using electricity if you leave them on standby!)
- using energy-saving bulbs instead of conventional filament bulbs
- using more efficient appliances (such as fridges, washing machines, etc.)
- using jug kettles, so you only heat the amount of water you need
- using timers to make sure electrical equipment is only turned on when it is needed
- using toasters instead of grills for making toast, and using microwave ovens instead of conventional ovens.

Reducing the use of fossil fuels

Burning fossil fuels is adding carbon dioxide to the atmosphere, and most scientists agree that this will make the Earth warm up and change the climate. We all need to reduce the amount of fossil fuels we use. As most of the electricity in the UK is generated by burning fossil fuels, reducing the amount of electricity we use (see above) will help.

We can also reduce the amounts of fossil fuels we use by:

- making sure our homes are well insulated
- setting the central heating thermostat lower and wearing more clothes at home
- walking or cycling for short journeys, and using public transport more often
- using more fuel-efficient cars when we cannot avoid driving
- buying electricity from companies that generate it using renewable resources.

?

5 Explain how these methods will help to reduce the amount of fossil fuels we burn.

[Total 5]

Summary

- Energy resources are divided into two main groups: renewable energy resources and non-renewable energy resources.
- Renewable energy resources will not run out while humans are living on Earth.
- There is only a limited supply of non-renewable energy resources. They cannot be replaced during the expected existence of humans on Earth.
- To preserve the Earth's valuable energy resources we need to use energy more efficiently and use as many renewable energy resources as possible.

Questions

1 _____ _____ are non-renewable energy resources. Solar power and biomass are examples of _____ energy resources. We need to _____ our use of energy to help reduce the emission of _____ gases and _____ the world's energy resources.

[Total 3]

2 a) Explain the difference between renewable and non-renewable energy resources. *[2]*
 b) Give three examples of each. *[6]*

[Total 8]

3 Explain how each of the following energy resources is dependent on the Sun:
 a) coal *[2]*
 b) wind energy *[2]*
 c) wave energy. *[2]*

[Total 6]

4 Draw up a table to show the advantages and disadvantages of each renewable energy resource.

[Total 4]

5 When Sarah was on holiday at a small hotel in Greece, she liked to get back to her room slightly early and have a shower before most of the other guests returned from the beach. Why might this be?

[Total 2]

6 A group of 30 people are going to set up a community on a small island off the coast of Scotland. They wish to become totally independent of the mainland within one year.
 a) List the possible energy resources that they may wish to use. *[3]*
 b) Write a letter to the community's 'energy resource working group'. Include advice on the energy resources that they should use, giving reasons for your recommendations. *[6]*

[Total 9]

The greenhouse effect

What is the 'greenhouse effect'?

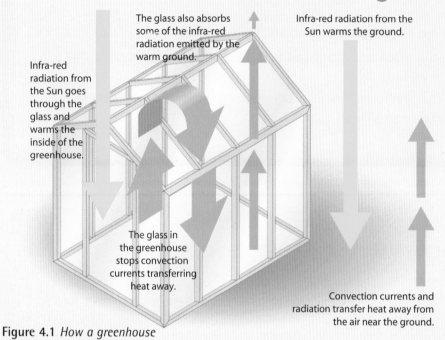

Infra-red radiation from the Sun goes through the glass and warms the inside of the greenhouse.

The glass also absorbs some of the infra-red radiation emitted by the warm ground.

Infra-red radiation from the Sun warms the ground.

The glass in the greenhouse stops convection currents transferring heat away.

Convection currents and radiation transfer heat away from the air near the ground.

Figure 4.1 *How a greenhouse works.*

Most scientists agree that adding carbon dioxide to the atmosphere is making the Earth warmer. This is sometimes referred to as the **'greenhouse effect'**. A greenhouse is being used as a model to help to explain how carbon dioxide warms the Earth. To understand the model, we first need to know how a greenhouse works.

Transparent materials such as glass or air do not absorb much of the infra-red radiation that arrives from the Sun. Other materials do absorb this radiation. Infra-red radiation is absorbed by the ground, and the ground warms up. The warm ground transfers thermal energy to the air above it, and this is how the air warms up in the sunshine.

How does the Earth warm up?

Everything gives out infra-red radiation. The hotter the object, the more infra-red radiation it gives out. Hotter objects also give out radiation with more energy than cooler objects. So the infra-red radiation coming from the Sun has more energy than the infra-red radiation emitted by the Earth. Most of this radiation passes through the atmosphere without being absorbed.

The Earth is much cooler than the Sun, so the infra-red radiation it emits has less energy. Some of the gases in the atmosphere can absorb some of this energy. Carbon dioxide is one of the **greenhouse gases** in the atmosphere that absorbs infra-red radiation from the Earth. The more carbon dioxide in the atmosphere, the more heat it absorbs. Figure 4.2 explains how this makes the Earth warm up.

?

1 List these things in order of how well they absorb infra-red radiation, starting with the best absorber: air, ground, glass.

[Total 3]

!

We need *some* carbon dioxide in our atmosphere. The average temperature of the Earth is approximately 14 °C. Without carbon dioxide in the atmosphere the Earth would be frozen over.

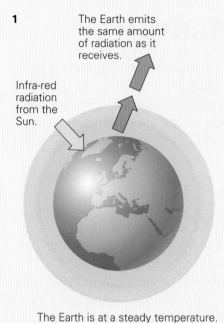

1 The Earth emits the same amount of radiation as it receives.

Infra-red radiation from the Sun.

The Earth is at a steady temperature.

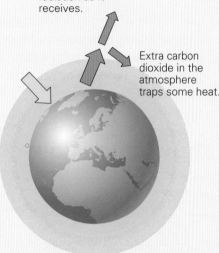

2 The Earth does not emits as much radiation as it receives.

Extra carbon dioxide in the atmosphere traps some heat.

The Earth is warming up.

3 The radiation that escapes from the atmosphere is the same as the amount of radiation received from the Sun.

The Earth is warmer, so it emits more radiation.

The Earth is at a new steady temperature.

Figure 4.2 *How the Earth warms up.*

Other greenhouse gases

Carbon dioxide is not the only gas in the atmosphere that absorbs infra-red radiation emitted by the Earth. Water vapour and methane are also important greenhouse gases. Some methane in the atmosphere comes from the digestive system of cows and other farm animals.

2 Write down three greenhouse gases.
[Total 3]

Questions

1 A greenhouse can be used as a model for the Earth and its atmosphere.
   a) Which part of the greenhouse represents 'greenhouse gases' in the atmosphere? *[1]*
   b) Explain how the model represents what happens in the atmosphere. *[2]*
   c) Are there any parts of the model that do not represent the Earth and atmosphere very well? *[2]*
   d) Do you think the model is useful in helping you to understand why carbon dioxide and other gases can make the Earth warmer? *[1]*
   [Total 6]

2 a) Suggest the main source of water vapour in the atmosphere. *[1]*
   b) Water vapour contributes more to the greenhouse effect than carbon dioxide. Why do you think that governments are not asking us to reduce the amount of water we are putting into the air? *[1]*
   [Total 2]

3 Many people are vegetarians because they believe that eating animals is wrong. However, being vegetarian could also help the environment. Suggest why this is. *[Total 2]*

Meeting the demand

The threat of global warming has led engineers to develop new ways of harnessing renewable energy resources, such as tidal-stream turbines and more efficient solar cells. We need **sustainable** energy resources if we are to reduce the amount of carbon dioxide we are putting into the atmosphere.

How much do we use?

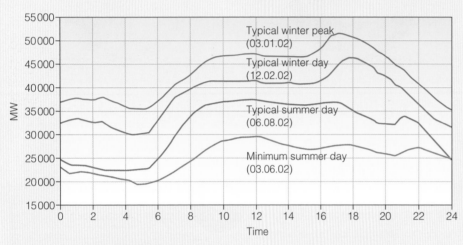

Figure 4.3 *How the demand for electricity varies between summer and winter.*

Figure 4.3 shows how the demand for electricity in the UK varies during the day and between summer and winter. The electricity supply companies need to be able to provide enough electricity to meet the demand. Electricity cannot be stored, so it has to be generated as it is needed.

A continuous supply

Fossil-fuelled power stations are so common because the fuel is relatively cheap (compared to the cost of generating the same amount of electricity using solar cells, for example), and they can provide power continuously.

Some renewable resources can also provide electricity continuously. These include geothermal and hydroelectric power stations and power stations that use biomass. However, there are not very many places in the UK (or even in the world) suitable for building the dams and reservoirs needed for hydroelectric power stations, and not many places suitable for geothermal power stations. If we tried to provide a large proportion of our electricity using biomass, we would have to use a lot of farmland for growing biomass crops, and food prices would go up. We would also need to clear large areas of forest around the world, which would harm wildlife. So we cannot generate enough continuous electricity using these renewable resources.

?

1 a) Name three fossil fuels used in power stations. [3]

b) What other non-renewable resource can be used to generate electricity? [1]

[Total 4]

Other renewable resources are not available continuously. Even worse, apart from tidal energy, we cannot predict exactly when they *will* be available. We will need to use a mix of different resources, but even this will probably not allow us to manage without burning fossil fuels.

2 Why do we need a way of generating electricity continuously?

[Total 1]

3 Why is it important that we use renewable energy resources wherever we can? [Total 2]

Figure 4.4 *Miscanthus grass can be grown in the UK as an 'energy crop'.*

Figure 4.5 *These floating devices are generating electricity as they bob up and down on the waves.*

Questions

1 Look at Figure 4.4.
   a) Suggest why the demand for electricity is greater in the winter than in the summer. [2]
   b) i) At what time of day is the demand for electricity highest?
      ii) Suggest why the demand is highest at this time. [2]
      [Total 4]

2 a) List the renewable energy resources that are not always available. [4]
   b) Which of these resources are most likely to be available in the winter? Explain your answer. [3]
      [Total 7]

3 We could grow a lot more crops for biomass fuels than we do at present.
   a) How would this help the environment? [1]
   b) How would this harm the environment? [1]
   c) How might this affect people in the developing world? [3]
      [Total 5]

4 The map shows the location of three different countries.

Figure 4.6 *Europe*

   a) Which renewable resources are not available in Austria? Explain your answer. [3]
   b) Which renewable resource will be more useful in Spain than in the UK or Austria? Explain your answer. [2]
      [Total 5]

Using radioactivity

What is radioactivity?

Most of the atoms that make up the things around us never change, although they can form different chemical compounds. However, some types of atom, such as the uranium used in nuclear reactors, can break up and form atoms of different elements. When atoms break up they give out radiation, which can consist of some of the tiny particles that make up atoms, or can be **gamma radiation**. Gamma radiation is similar to light and infra-red radiation, but it transfers a lot more energy.

Discovery

Radioactivity was discovered in 1896, by the French physicist Henri Becquerel (1852–1908). He was investigating some uranium salts, which he placed on a photographic plate wrapped in black paper. He later found that there was an image on the plate. He carried out further tests, and concluded that the uranium salts had emitted some kind of radiation that had affected the plate.

Marie Curie (1867–1934) and her husband Pierre (1859–1906) followed up this discovery by investigating ores of uranium. By careful measurement, they found that these ores emitted more radiation than could be explained by the uranium in them. They eventually discovered two new radioactive elements in the ores: polonium and radium. The Curies and Becquerel shared the Nobel Prize for Physics in 1903 for their discoveries.

Early uses

When radium was first discovered, people thought that this wonderful new material would be able to cure various health problems. Some manufacturers added it to items like toothpaste and even to food. The energy given off by radium as it changed made a glow, and so radium was used in 'glow in the dark' paint, on items such as watches.

In the 1920s, workers in factories that made these watches began to report problems with their teeth and jaws. They licked their brushes to make the points fine enough to paint thin lines on the factory's products. It was discovered that the radium in the paint they were using was causing their problems, and eventually the use of radium was banned.

Figure 4.7 *Marie Curie at work in her lab.*

! The Curies had to refine tonnes of pitchblende (uranium ore) to obtain just a few grams of radium.

? **1** What evidence made the Curies start to look for new elements in uranium ores? *[Total 7]*

Figure 4.8 *A watch with luminous hands on the face.*

Modern uses

Today there are many more radioactive materials known, and they are used for scientific research and in medicine. There are strict safety rules governing the use of all radioactive substances, as exposure to radiation can cause cancer and other health problems. However radiation is also very useful. It can be used to treat cancer, and to investigate various illnesses.

Any new substance discovered today would have to be thoroughly investigated to find out if it was safe before it could be used in consumer products.

> **!** No one knew about the dangers of radioactivity when it was first discovered, so the early scientists all worked without safety precautions. Marie Curie's laboratory notebooks are still so radioactive that they are kept in lead-lined boxes.

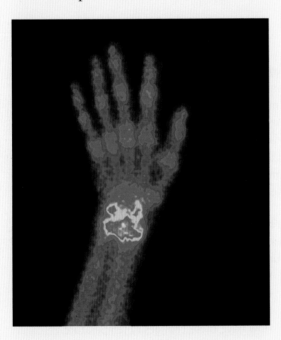

Figure 4.9 *A radioactive tracer has been injected into this patient. It concentrates in areas where the bones are abnormal and the gamma rays it gives off are detected by a special camera. This patient has damage in her left wrist*

Figure 4.10 *Radiation hazard symbol.*

Questions

1 a) Name one material that can act as a shield against radioactivity.   [1]
   b) Explain how you worked out your answer.   [2]
       [Total 3]

2 Imagine that a new chemical was discovered today, and manufacturers wanted to use it in face creams.
   a) Suggest what would have to happen before they were allowed to sell creams using this new chemical.   [3]

   b) How do you think this is different to the way new chemicals were used in the 1900s? Explain your answer.   [3]
       [Total 6]

3 Many people who work with radioactive materials wear film badges. Find out what a film badge is, and how it helps workers to stay safe.   [Total 4]

End of section questions

1 Write down the names of five things in your home that transfer energy from one form to another. Next to each one write down the energy transfers that take place. *[Total 5]*

2 a) Copy and complete the diagram of a moving car shown in Figure 1. *[8]*

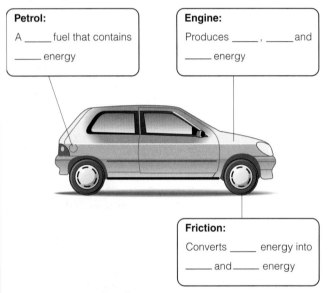

Petrol:

A _____ fuel that contains _____ energy

Engine:

Produces _____ , _____ and _____ energy

Friction:

Converts _____ energy into _____ and _____ energy

Figure 1

b) Draw a flow diagram to show the energy changes taking place when a car is travelling up a hill. *[4]*

[Total 12]

3 What is meant by the law of conservation of energy? *[Total 2]*

4 An electric motor is 20% efficient at transferring electrical energy into kinetic energy. 75% of the electrical energy supplied to the motor is transferred to thermal energy and the rest is transferred to sound energy. Copy and complete the Sankey diagram for this electric motor. *[Total 3]*

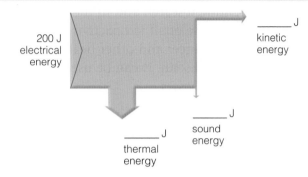

200 J electrical energy

_____ J kinetic energy

_____ J sound energy

_____ J thermal energy

Figure 2

5 Owen eats a medium sized bar of chocolate that contains 1000 kJ of chemical energy. When climbing 1 m up a ladder Owen will convert 500 J of chemical energy into potential energy.
How high up the ladder would Owen have to climb to use up all the energy in the chocolate bar? (Ignore the energy he would convert to thermal energy and remember 1 kJ = 1000 J). *[Total 3]*

6 To hammer a horseshoe into shape a blacksmith heats it until it is red hot. The blacksmith then plunges it into cold water.
a) What happens to the temperature of the horseshoe and the temperature of the water? *[2]*
b) How have these changes in temperature taken place? *[2]*

[Total 4]

7 Explain the following terms:
a) heat conduction *[3]*
b) convection *[3]*
c) heat radiation. *[3]*

[Total 9]

8 If you open the door of a fridge, your feet will feel colder than the top of your legs. Use ideas about convection and particles to explain this. *[Total 3]*

9 Use your understanding of particles to explain the difference between a saucepan of water boiling dry on a stove and a puddle on the pavement evaporating. *[Total 4]*

10 Hajar carried out an investigation to compare the rate of heat loss from two different kinds of take-away cup. She poured very hot water into each of them and recorded the temperature every five minutes. The results are shown in Table 1.

Table 1 *Temperatures of water in different cups.*

Time (min)	0	5	10	15	20	25	30
Polystyrene cup with lid (°C)	84	67	54	43	34	28	22
Paper cup without lid (°C)	96	72	54	41	37	23	17

a) Plot the two sets of data on one graph. *[6]*
b) Write a conclusion for Hajar's experiment. *[3]*
c) Explain what you think Hajar may have done wrong and suggest how she could improve her experiment. *[3]*
[Total 12]

11 Table 2 shows the consumption of energy resources in different regions around the world in 2007. The figures are in millions of tonnes of oil equivalent.

Table 2

Region	Oil	Gas	Coal	Hydroelectric	Nuclear
North America	1135	729	613	146	216
Latin America	252	121	22	153	4
Europe	949	1040	534	189	276
Middle East	295	269	6	5	0
Africa	138	75	106	22	3
Asia and Australasia	1185	403	1896	194	123

Source: BP Statistical review.

a) Which region uses the most oil? *[1]*
b) Which region uses more fossil fuels than any other region? *[1]*
c) Suggest why the Middle East only uses a small amount of hydroelectric energy. *[2]*
d) Draw a bar chart to show energy consumption within Europe. *[6]*
e) Which of these energy resources are contributing to global warming? Explain your answer. *[2]*
[Total 12]

12 A bicycle can be powered by solar energy by using solar cells to charge batteries. When the batteries are fully charged they can then be used to power a motor on the front wheel.
a) What energy transfers are taking place when the batteries are being charged? *[2]*

b) Describe the energy transfers taking place when the motor is being used. Include wasted energy transfers in your answer. *[4]*
[Total 6]

13
P Plan an investigation to find out if shiny surfaces radiate more or less heat than dull surfaces.

14
R Carry out an electrical energy survey at home.
a) What methods of saving electrical energy do you and your family already use?
b) How could you reduce the amount of electrical energy that your family uses?

15
R Write an article for a local newspaper explaining the advantages and the disadvantages of building a wind farm in your area. Include possible locations where a wind farm may be built, and why we cannot rely on wind energy to supply our electricity.

2.1 Light

Why can you hear your friends if they are standing round a corner but you cannot see them? What form of energy enables you to read this page? Light enables us to see but you cannot see something unless light is shining on it.

Light

Light is the form of energy which enables us to see objects, as our eyes are sensitive to it. It is part of the **electromagnetic spectrum** and travels at a speed of 300 000 000 m/s (see Section 4.1 for a definition of speed).

Sound is very slow compared with light. It travels at only 330 m/s. If you are watching a race you can see the smoke from the starting pistol before you hear the sound. Thunder and lightning happen at the same time. You see the lightning before you hear the thunder. This is because sound travels so much slower than light. You can roughly estimate how far away a thunderstorm is by counting the number of seconds between the lightning flash and the thunder. The larger the number you count the further away the storm is. The storm will be 1 km away for every three seconds that you count.

Light is an energy wave. This type of wave is called a **transverse wave** and all the forms of energy in the electromagnetic spectrum travel this way.

> **!** Light from the Sun takes 8 minutes to reach the Earth. If you travelled in a car at over 160 km/h it would take you more than a hundred years to cover the same distance.

> **!** Lightning flashes can be 30 km long.

> **?** 1 What is the speed of light in km/h?
> [Total 2]

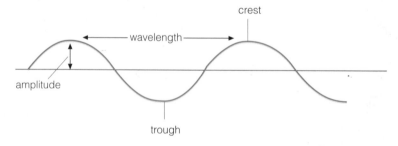

Figure 1.1 *A transverse wave.*

Luminous and illuminated

Imagine being in a very dark cave. It is impossible to see anything unless you strike a match or turn on a torch. The match and the torch give off their own light: they are called **luminous** objects. Your computer screen or a burning candle are also luminous objects. The light from these will hit other things around you and bounce into your eyes. This light will illuminate these things and you will be able to see them. Some source of light is illuminating the page you are reading.

The stars are luminous but the planets and the Moon are **illuminated** by light from our star, the Sun. Moonlight is really light reflected from the Sun. Jupiter and Venus can be seen at night because they are illuminated by the Sun and reflect the light.

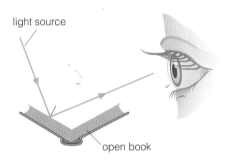

Figure 1.2 *The light is hitting the object and reflecting into the eye.*

Rectilinear propagation

A car headlight will not light the road round a corner. This is because light travels in straight lines. We call this **rectilinear propagation**. In Figure 1.3 you can see the light travelling out from behind the trees. Can you think of any other way to show that light travels in straight lines?

Shadows

You cannot see through a brick wall. This is because the brick will not allow light to go through it. It is **opaque** to light. Windows will allow light to go through them: they are **transparent**. A frosted bathroom window will let some light through. It is **translucent**.

Figure 1.3 *Light travels in straight lines.*

The shadow of the palm tree on this beach is fuzzy, because the top of the tree is several metres above the sand. If you were to hold your hand out just above the sand, the shadow of your hand would be clear and sharp.

Figure 1.4 *The tree is blocking the light and casting a shadow onto the sand.*

?

2 Which of the following are luminous?
a) cat
b) torch (swiched on!)
c) Halley's comet
d) a stained glass window
[Total 4]

3 How does an umbra shadow show that light travels in straight lines?

[Total 2]

Figure 1.5a shows a clear dark shadow is being cast on the screen. This is because the object is stopping all the light and only light round the edge is hitting the screen. This type of shadow is an **umbra**.

If the light source is large in comparison with the object, some of the light around the edges is getting past the object and the shadow is no longer clear and sharp. The grey fuzzy shadow is called the **penumbra**.

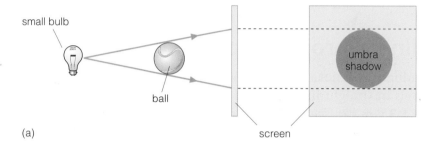

(a)

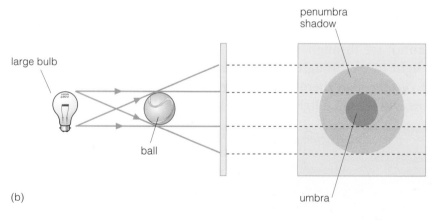

(b)

Figure 1.5 *The formation of an a) umbra and b) penumbra.*

Summary

- Light is part of the electromagnetic spectrum.
- A luminous object gives off its own light.
- An object that reflects light is visible when illuminated.
- Light travels in straight lines.
- Light travels very much faster (300 000 000 m/s) than sound (330 m/s).
- Light is reflected off objects into our eyes.
- Opaque objects can block light and cast shadows.

Questions

1 Copy and complete the following sentences. Light is a form of _____. A wooden door will not let light through as it is _____. A glass window is _____ because it will let light through. You can see the Moon at night because light from the Sun _____ from it.
[Total 2]

2 a) Which of the following sentences are correct? *[3]*
   i) You can see the light from a firework before you hear the sound.
   ii) The Moon is illuminated.
   iii) Light can travel round corners.
   iv) A fuzzy grey shadow is called a penumbra.
   v) Tracing paper is transparent.
b) For each statement that is incorrect, say what is wrong. Rewrite the statement to make it correct.
[2]
[Total 5]

3 Why do you always see lightning before you hear the thunder?
[Total 2]

4 Your friends are standing round a corner. Why are they not visible?
[Total 2]

5 Sally is walking towards a spotlight on the wall of her house. She is casting a shadow across the garden. What will happen to the shadow as she moves towards the house?
[Total 2]

6 a) You could use sunlight and a mirror to send messages. How could you do this?
[2]
b) Can you think of any other object that would work using sunlight?
[1]
[Total 3]

7 a) Light travels faster than sound. Describe how you could show this to a friend.
[2]
b) How could you show your friend that light travels in straight lines?
[2]
[Total 4]

8 a) Light travels at 300 000 km/s. It takes light 8.33 min to reach Earth from the Sun. Work out how far away the Sun is.
[2]
b) The reflected light from the Moon takes only 1.3 s to reach Earth. How far is the Moon from the Earth?
[2]
[Total 4]

9 a) What is rectilinear propagation?
[1]
b) Give two examples that illustrate rectilinear propagation.
[2]
[Total 3]

10 If you are counting the number of seconds between lightning and thunder, explain why every three seconds is a kilometre of distance to the storm.
[Total 3]

2.2 Reflection

Why can you see your face in a mirror but not in a wall? How can we make light go round corners? This page is reflecting light into your eyes. It is not shiny because not all the light is reaching your eyes. If you had a mirror on the table next to the book, the mirror would look much shinier.

Reflection

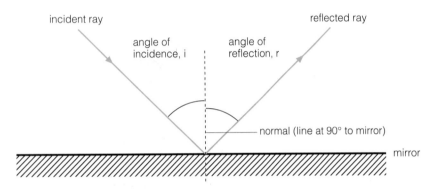

Figure 2.1 shows how light is reflected into your eyes from a mirror.

A line can be drawn at right angles to the mirror where the ray hits the mirror – it is called the **normal**. The light going towards the mirror is the **incident ray**. The angle between the normal and the incident ray is called the **angle of incidence**. The light coming away from the mirror is the **reflected ray**. The angle between the normal and the reflected ray is called the **angle of reflection**. The two angles are equal to each other.

Figure 2.1 *Reflection of light from a smooth surface*

> The angle of incidence is equal to the angle of reflection

Rough and smooth surfaces

The page you are reading does not shine because it has a very rough surface when magnified. The light hitting the page is scattered and only some light enters your eyes. This is called **diffuse reflection**. Many surfaces are rough which is why they look dull even in bright light.

A mirror is much smoother and will reflect light in a regular way so that much more light will enter your eyes. This is called **regular reflection**. When you look into a mirror, all the light is reflected so you get an **image** of your face.

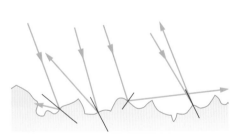

Figure 2.2 *The reflection of light from a rough surface.*

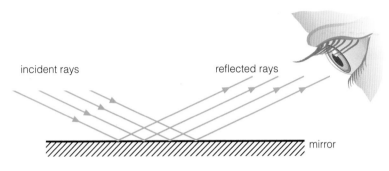

incident rays   reflected rays

mirror

Figure 2.3 *The regular reflection of light.*

Virtual reality is like your image in a mirror. It does not exist, it only appears to be real.

A wall is rough so most of the light never reaches your eyes and cannot form an image. Images can be seen in many places, for example, in still water or polished metal.

Reflection in a mirror

When you see a reflection of yourself in a plane mirror you expect the reflection to be the same size and colour as you. What is different is that the image is back to front or **laterally inverted**. Some images like the ones in a cinema can be projected onto a screen. They are **real** images. Your image in the mirror only seems to be there, but you could not produce it on a screen. It is a **virtual** image.

Seeing round corners

Light travels in straight lines so you cannot see round corners unless you use mirrors to help. Figure 2.5 shows a **periscope**. If the light hits the first mirror at an angle of 45° then the angle of reflection will also be 45°. The ray of light will have been turned through 90°. When the light hits the second mirror, it is reflected back through 90°. The periscope can be used to see round corners or over an object blocking your view.

Figure 2.4 *You do not really exist behind the mirror. Your reflection is virtual.*

Figure 2.5 *The arrangement of mirrors in a periscope which enables us to see round corners.*

Summary

- Light is reflected from a surface.
- The angle of incidence equals the angle of reflection.
- The image in a mirror is back to front (laterally inverted).
- The image in a mirror is the same size and colour as the object.
- Smooth surfaces reflect more regularly than rougher surfaces.
- A periscope will reflect light and let you see round corners.

Questions

1 Copy and complete the following sentences. The image in a mirror does not exist. It is _____. The image in a mirror is the same shape, size and _____ as the object. The angle of _____ equals the angle of _____. A line drawn at 90° to a mirror is called a _____. A rough surfaces gives _____ reflection. *[Total 3]*

2 Ben is towing a caravan and finds that he cannot see the road behind him. Draw a way to help him using mirrors. He cannot use mirrors any bigger than his wing mirrors. *[Total 4]*

3 A beam of white light shines onto a sheet of white paper. An identical beam of light shines onto a mirror. Describe how the scattering by paper and the reflection by a mirror are different from each other. *[Total 4]*

4 a) Work out the angle of reflection shown in Figure 2.6. *[1]*
b) What is the total angle turned by the light. *[1]*
[Total 2]

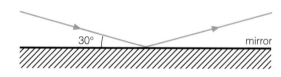

Figure 2.6

5 a) Sam sits in an optician's chair and looks at the chart in a mirror in front of him. He needs to be able to read the letters. They are all capital letters and Sam is seeing them in a mirror. Why will some letters look incorrect? *[2]*
b) Write down **two** capital letters which will not be affected. *[2]*
[Total 4]

6 The driveway at Dina's house leads out onto a blind corner. She needs some help to see cars on the road when she leaves the driveway in her car. Using one or two mirrors draw a plan of what she can do. *[Total 3]*

2.3 Refraction

Why does a swimming pool never look as deep as it is? Why does a straw in a glass of water always look bent? What makes a diamond sparkle? Light changes direction as it goes from air into glass or water. This principle has many applications.

Light travels in air at a speed of 300 000 000 m/s but if the light goes into a substance or **medium** which is optically denser than air it slows down. The light seems to bend. This is called **refraction**.

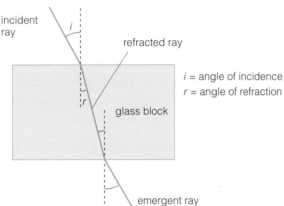

incident ray

i

refracted ray

i = angle of incidence
r = angle of refraction

r

glass block

emergent ray

Figure 3.1 *How light bends as it travels from air to glass.*

The ray of light hitting the glass is the incident ray. The angle between the normal and the incident ray forms the angle of incidence. The light entering the glass is the **refracted ray**. The angle of incidence is larger than the angle of refraction as the ray of light bends towards the normal. The light is slowing down because glass is optically denser than air. When the light leaves the glass the angle of incidence is now smaller than the angle of refraction as the ray of light bends away from the normal. The light is speeding up because air is optically less dense than glass.

> When light travels from a less to a more optically dense medium it refracts *towards* the normal. When light travels from a more to a less dense medium it refracts *away* from the normal.

? 1 Explain why angle *r* is smaller than angle *i* in Figure 3.1. [Total 2]

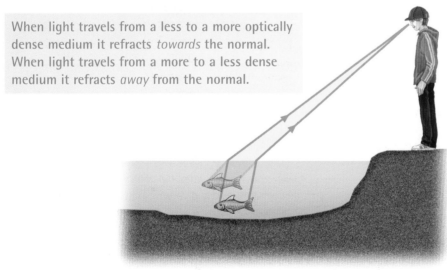

Figure 3.2 *The fish is not really where the person sees it because the water refracts the light.*

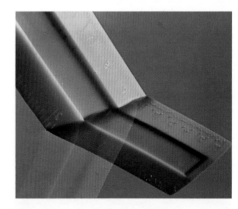

Can you explain why this ruler appears to bend in the water? What trick is being played on our eyes?

2 Light and sound

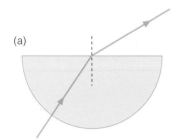

A swimming pool is always deeper than it looks.

The critical angle for glass/air is 42° and the critical angle for water/air is 49°.

Look at Figure 3.2. It only appears that the fish is in a different place and that the ruler is bent. They are optical illusions caused by refraction. The things in the diagrams only appear to happen. Your eyes assume that light travels in straight lines and sees the optical illusions even though your brain knows the truth.

Total internal reflection

Figure 3.3 shows light being refracted in a semi-circular glass block. If the angle of incidence is gradually increased the light will eventually have nowhere to refract to and **total internal reflection** takes place (Figure 3.3b and c). This happens when the light has reached the **critical angle** although some internal reflection will take place before that.

If the incident ray goes through the curved surface it will not refract because it is hitting the surface at 90° and refraction will not occur.

Prisms

Figure 3.4 shows two 45° angle prisms and how they are used in periscopes, and cat's eyes. Precious stones are cut so that the flat surfaces act like prisms and reflect light.

(a)
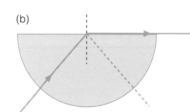

(b)

(c)
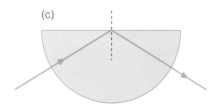

below the critical angle; b) angle of incidence is at the critical angle; c) angle of incidence is greater than the critical angle – total internal reflection takes place.

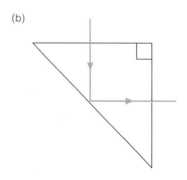

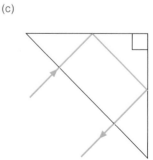

Figure 3.4 *Prisms in use:*
  a) precious stone.   *b) prism used in a periscope*   *c) prism used in cat's eyes*

42

If the angle of incidence is greater than the critical angle for glass then total internal reflection takes place. The light can be turned through an angle of 90° or 180°.

Total internal reflection is used in cat's eyes on roads, the cut of precious stones and light guides. Light guides can be made small enough to enter the human body. This enables a doctor to look inside the body to save the patient major surgery. These are called **endoscopes**.

> **!** The halo that you sometimes see around the Moon is caused by moonlight refracting inside tiny ice crystals high in the Earth's atmosphere.

Lenses

Lenses are transparent and can change the direction of light.

The lens in Figure 3.5 is fatter in the middle and will magnify an image. If it is used to produce an image on a screen, the image will be upside down. When the image is sharp and clear we say it is in focus. Your eye lens and the lens in a camera are this shape. It is called a **convex** lens.

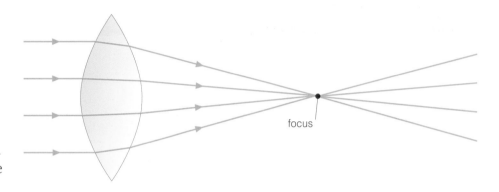

Figure 3.5 *A convex lens.*

The lens in Figure 3.6 is thinner in the middle and gives a small, upright image. If you cannot see distant objects and need to wear spectacles the lenses will be like this. It is called a **concave** lens.

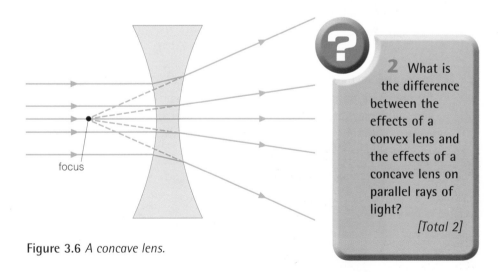

Figure 3.6 *A concave lens.*

> **?** **2** What is the difference between the effects of a convex lens and the effects of a concave lens on parallel rays of light?
>
> [Total 2]

Summary

- Light slows down when travelling into a more optically dense medium.
- Light speeds up when entering a less optically dense medium.
- The bending of light is called refraction.
- Total internal reflection occurs when the angle of incidence reaches the critical angle for the boundary between substances.

Questions

1 Copy and complete the following sentences. When light travels from air into glass the light will bend. This is called _____. The light will bend _____ the normal. When light goes from water to air it will bend _____ _____ the normal. In special circumstances the light does not bend but bounces back. This is called _____ _____ _____.

[Total 3]

2 Look at Figure 3.7. Can Samantha see the object at the bottom of the swimming pool? Copy the diagram and add the rays of light. *[Total 2]*

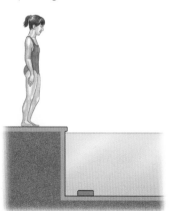

Figure 3.7

3 Imagine that you are a fish underwater. When you look up to the surface of the water you can see the sky and also the bottom of the pool. Try to explain this unusual view. A ray diagram might help.

[Total 3]

4 Tom wants to bend a ray of light round a corner but he does not have a mirror, only a prism shaped piece of glass. Draw a diagram to show how he could bend the light round the corner. Add the ray of light to your diagram. *[Total 4]*

5 Raj puts a rectangular glass block onto a mirror.
   a) Draw a diagram of this seen from the side. *[1]*
   b) Put in a ray of light shining from the left of your diagram through the glass block and onto the mirror. *[1]*
   c) Put in the reflected and refracted rays. *[2]*

[Total 4]

6 Why do spear fishermen have to aim below the fish they want to catch? *[Total 2]*

7 Why is the critical angle for water greater than the critical angle for glass? *[Total 2]*

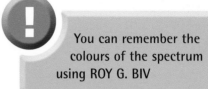

2.4 Colour

How do we get the colours of the rainbow? Why do objects look coloured? How can we change the colour of an object just by using light?

White light is made up of the seven colours of the **spectrum**:

- red
- orange
- yellow
- green
- blue
- indigo
- violet.

> **!** You can remember the colours of the spectrum using ROY G. BIV

> **?** 1 Write down your own idea for a way to remember the order of the colours of the spectrum.
> *[Total 2]*

Why do we get all the colours?

With our eyes it is not possible to see the colours in white light. When the light goes into a **prism** each colour is slowed down by a slightly different amount. This means they refract by different amounts and spread out so we can see the colours. Red light travels faster in glass than blue light. Red light does not refract as much.

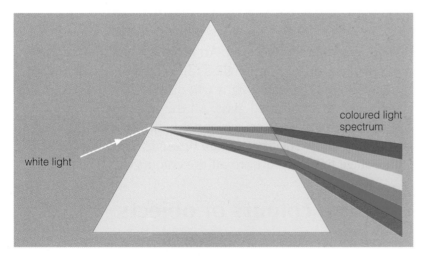
white light
coloured light spectrum

Figure 4.1 *White light can be split into the colours of the spectrum using a prism.*

> **!** When a rainbow forms, water droplets in the air are acting like prisms.

Coloured objects

A banana looks yellow because the pigment in the skin of the banana will only reflect yellow light. All the other colours are absorbed. A piece of charcoal looks black because it will not reflect any of the colours. They are all absorbed. This white paper will reflect all the colours of light. The black letters do not reflect any of the colours.

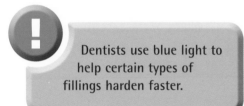

Dentists use blue light to help certain types of fillings harden faster.

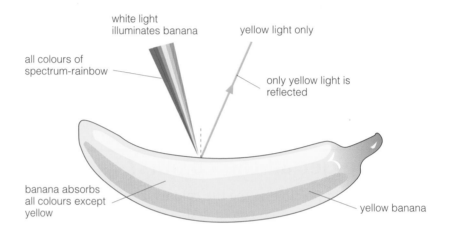

Figure 4.2 *White light is hitting the banana but only yellow is reflected.*

Coloured filters

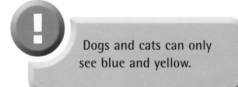

Coloured filters do not add colour to white light. They filter out the colours in the white light leaving the colour we see.

Traffic lights are green, amber and red. An ordinary light bulb is used behind coloured glass. The coloured glass filters out some colours. The red dye in the glass of a red traffic light will only let the red part of the spectrum go through the coloured glass. All the other colours are absorbed. In a disco or at a concert, coloured lights are created using filters that will only allow specific colours through. The blue dye in a filter on a blue stage light will absorb all the colours except blue.

Changing the colours of objects

Dogs and cats can only see blue and yellow.

Why do you think it is so important to have the whitest spotlights possible at a football match?

Sam and Ellen are at a disco. Sam is wearing blue trousers and a yellow top. Ellen is wearing a red top and green trousers. Look at Figure 4.3. In blue light, only Sam's trousers look blue. Sam's top looks black because it will only reflect yellow light and no light is reflected when blue light shines on it. Ellen's clothes also look black. Her trousers only reflect green light and her top only reflects red light. In blue light neither the trousers nor the shirt will reflect any light. What colour would Sam and Ellen's clothes look in red light and green light?

The same thing will happen to football strips. If one team in a football match was playing in a white strip and the other team was playing in a yellow strip, and yellow floodlights were used, there would be some confusion. You would not be able to tell the difference between the two teams as both strips would appear to be the same colour.

2 Explain why carrots look orange.

[Total 1]

3 What colour would a carrot look under a blue light?

[Total 1]

Figure 4.3 *Sam and Ellen in white light and blue light.*

Summary

- White light is made up of seven colours.
- Light can be split into its colours using a prism.
- White surfaces reflect all the colours.
- Coloured filters will absorb all the colours except the colour of the dye in them.
- Objects reflect the colour of the pigment they contain.
- If all the colours are absorbed an object looks black.

Questions

1 Copy and complete the following sentences :-
The seven colours of the spectrum are red,
_____, yellow, _____,
_____, indigo and _____. A blue
light shining through a red filter will give
_____. A white shirt with a red light on it
will look _____. In yellow light, black shorts
will look _____. In red light, a blue shirt will
look _____.   *[Total 4]*

2 You see a car accident at night and yellow sodium
lamps illuminate the streets. Why would it be very
difficult for you to tell the police what the colour of
the cars were that were involved in the accident?
                                                [Total 4]

3 It is a sunny day and you have decided to wear some
blue tinted sunglasses. You go to cross the road but
are unsure if the crossing light is red or green. What
is causing the problem and what might you see?
                                                [Total 4]

4 a) A stage director is very concerned about the
stage lighting changing the colour of the actors'
clothes. He says that if they all wear white there
will not be a problem when the lights change
colour because the clothes will still look white. Is
he right?   *[2]*
b) What might you suggest and why?   *[2]*
                                                [Total 4]

5 How is a rainbow formed?   *[Total 3]*

6 a) White light shines into a prism and forms a
spectrum on a screen. What effect, if any, would
you see if a red filter were placed in the path of
the white light?   *[2]*
b) Would it make any difference if the filter were
placed at the other side of the prism near the
screen?   *[1]*
c) The screen is changed to a green one. What might
you see now?   *[2]*
[Total 5]

7 a) If you are riding your bike at night, it is sensible
to wear clothing with reflective strips. How do
these work?   *[2]*
b) Is white or black clothing a more sensible choice
when riding your bike? Give a reason for your
answer.
                                               [3]
                                               [Total 5]

8 On a sunny day, why might you expect a zebra's skin
to warm up unevenly?   *[Total 2]*

9 When it is freshly picked, a banana is green. Over
time it turns yellow, and eventually goes black.
Explain how the reflection of light from the banana
changes as it ages.
                                               [Total 4]

2.5 Hearing and sound

Can sound travel through anything? What causes a sound to be produced? How can sound be changed? Sound waves are different to light waves – they have different properties.

You have probably produced a sound by stretching an elastic band across your fingers and plucking it. The tighter the elastic band the higher the note produced. If you pluck it really hard the noise is much louder. You can do the same thing with a ruler over the edge of a bench. Try to work out how to make the noise louder or higher.

Sound production

For a sound to be produced something needs to **vibrate** to produce the sound. When you talk air passing over your vocal cords makes them vibrate to give the sound of your voice. When a sound is produced the **molecules** in the air carry the sound from one place to another by squeezing together (**compression**) and moving apart (**rarefaction**). These moving molecules carry the sound energy. If there are no molecules then sound cannot be transmitted. Sound cannot travel through a vacuum but it can travel through gases, liquids and solids.

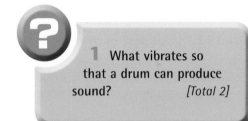

? 1 What vibrates so that a drum can produce sound? *[Total 2]*

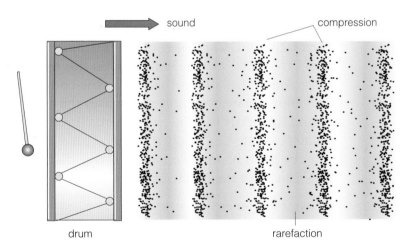

Figure 5.1 *Sound waves travel through the air from the drum in a series of compressions and rarefactions.*

! You will never hear an explosion in space because there are no molecules to carry the sound.

The closer together the molecules are, the faster the sound will travel because the molecules do not have to move very far to hit another one. Sound energy will be transmitted more rapidly in water than in

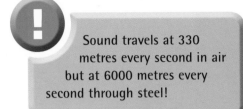

Sound travels at 330 metres every second in air but at 6000 metres every second through steel!

air because the molecules in water are much closer together than they are in air.

Looking at a sound wave

Figure 5.2 shows a sound wave as seen on an oscilloscope which is connected to a microphone. The low points are called **troughs**; they represent the rarefaction on a sound wave. The high points are **crests** and these represent the compressions. The distance between two crests or two troughs is called the **wavelength** and is measured in metres. The height of a crest or the depth of a trough is called the **amplitude**. If you were to stand at one end of the wave and count how many waves passed you in one second then you would have measured the **frequency** of the wave. The units of frequency are cycles per second or **hertz (Hz)**.

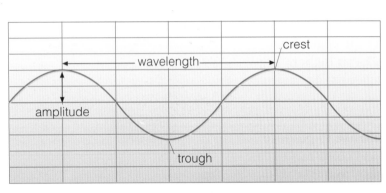

Figure 5.2 *A sound wave as shown on an oscilloscope.*

Pitch and loudness

The larger the amplitude of the vibrations the louder the sound. The closer together the vibrations, the higher the frequency, and the higher pitched the sound is.

Musical instruments rely on vibration to produce a regular sound. Something in the instrument causes the air to vibrate. With a violin it is the movement of the strings that makes the body of the violin vibrate, which in turn makes the air around it vibrate. In wind instruments the air is made to vibrate in a wooden or metal tube. To raise the pitch of a note on a violin you change one or more of the following things:

- use a lighter weight string
- make the string shorter
- put more tension in the string.

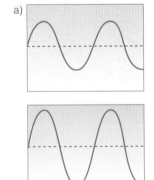
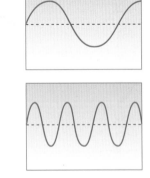

Figure 5.3 *a) Two sounds with the same pitch, but the one at the bottom is louder. b) Two sounds with the same loudness, but the one at the bottom has a higher pitch.*

Detecting sound – the ear

The ear is a very complex organ consisting of three main sections. The main parts of the ear are the **outer ear** which collects the vibrations and directs them to the **middle ear**. In the middle ear the vibrations are picked up by the **eardrum**, which transmits this movement to the small bones called the **hammer**, **anvil** and **stirrup**. These magnify the vibrations and send them to the **inner ear** where the fluid inside the **cochlea** starts to move and stimulates the nerve endings. The nerves carry the information to the brain and you recognise this as a sound.

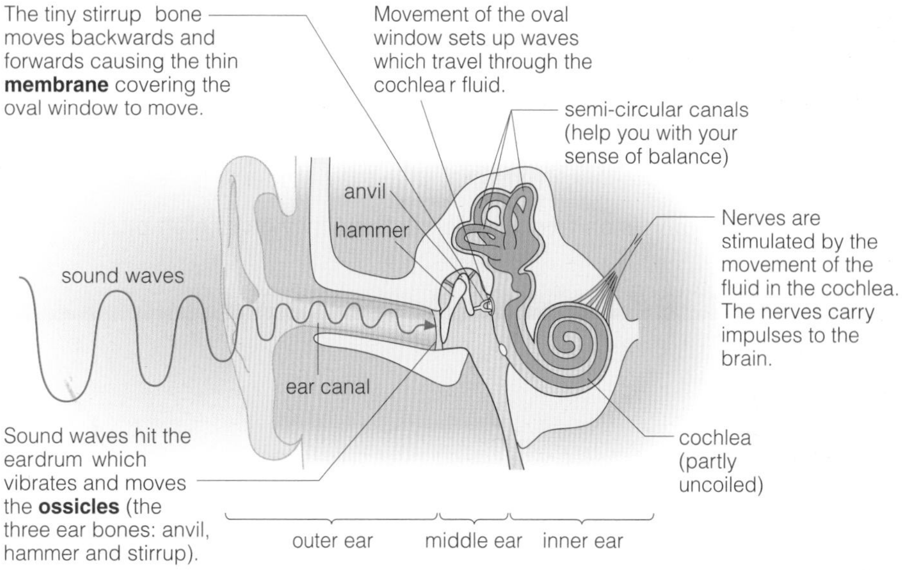

The tiny stirrup bone moves backwards and forwards causing the thin **membrane** covering the oval window to move.

Movement of the oval window sets up waves which travel through the cochlea r fluid.

semi-circular canals (help you with your sense of balance)

anvil

hammer

sound waves

Nerves are stimulated by the movement of the fluid in the cochlea. The nerves carry impulses to the brain.

ear canal

Sound waves hit the eardrum which vibrates and moves the **ossicles** (the three ear bones: anvil, hammer and stirrup).

cochlea (partly uncoiled)

outer ear   middle ear   inner ear

Figure 5.4 *The ear.*

The hearing range for humans is from about 20 Hz to about 20 000 Hz. As you get older you cannot hear sounds at the lower and upper end of the range.

If the vibrations become too loud then they can damage your eardrum. People working with loud noise all day need to protect their ears from too much sound energy. If you stand too close to a loudspeaker at a concert this can cause temporary deafness. This is because the nerve endings in the cochlea stop working properly for a while. This temporary deafness will wear off after about an hour. If you continue to damage the nerve endings with, say, a personal stereo with the volume too loud, then the deafness will become permanent.

Sometimes the vibration of the sound wave can be so large it will tear or cause a hole in your eardrum. This is called a perforated eardrum and your hearing will be permanently impaired. Noise-induced deafness cannot be cured.

Any sound which is unpleasant to someone is called a **noise**. A noise for one person may be excellent music to someone else!

Sound levels are measured in **decibels (dB)** using a sound meter. Anything above 130 dB will hurt your ears to listen to and could cause permanent damage.

! A dog can hear up to 40 000 Hz, which is twice as high as any human, and a bat can hear up to 100 000 Hz.

! The noise level in a quiet classroom may be about 40 dB. If the teacher leaves the room the noise level may rise to as much as 80 dB.

Summary

- Vibrating molecules carry sound energy.
- Sound needs a substance to carry it.
- Sound travels faster if the molecules of the medium it is travelling through are closer together.
- The higher the amplitude of a sound the louder it is.
- Pitch depends on frequency. High frequency gives high pitch.

Questions

1 Copy and complete the following sentences.
Sound is heard because our _____ vibrates.
Sound can travel through solids _____ and
_____. Sound is measured in _____.
High _____ of vibration makes a
_____ pitched sound.   *[Total 3]*

2 a) Which of the following statements are correct? *[3]*
   i) To produce a sound something must vibrate.
   ii) Sound can travel easily through a vacuum.
   iii) You could talk to your friend on the Moon.
   iv) Air carries sound by a system of compressions
       and rarefactions.
   v) Very loud noise can damage your ears.
   b) For each statement that is incorrect, say what is
      wrong. Rewrite the statement to make it correct.
                                                        [2]
                                                   [Total 5]

3 Native Americans could hear horses approaching by
putting their ears to the ground. Can you explain
why this worked?   *[Total 2]*

4 When people are working in a noisy factory they
need to protect their hearing. Suggest ways they
could do this.   *[Total 3]*

5 Hares can communicate to other hares by stamping
their feet to warn of danger. How do you think this
works?   *[Total 2]*

6 Why would a perforated eardrum impair your
hearing?   *[Total 2]*

7
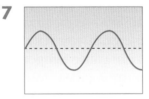 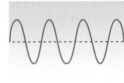

Figure 5.5 *a) and b) Oscilloscope traces of
different sounds.*

Figure 5.5 shows oscilloscope traces for two sounds.
How would the two sounds have sounded different?
                                                   [Total 4]

2.6 Reflection of sound

How can echoes help us to 'see' things? Sound reflects off surfaces. Sometimes this can be annoying, but at other times we can make use of echoes.

Echoes

If you stand in an empty room and make a noise the sound seems to bounce off the walls. The sound waves are being reflected in just the same way as light and we call this an **echo**. A room with curtains and carpets does not sound the same because the furnishings will **absorb** some of the sound energy.

Some animals use sound to help them 'see' in the dark or under water. We call this **echolocation**. Bats are very good at using echolocation and they can even catch fast flying insects this way. They emit high-pitched sound waves which bounce of objects. The bat uses the echo to determine where the object is. Human beings have developed machines which use echoes to locate shoals of fish or submarines under water and oil under ground.

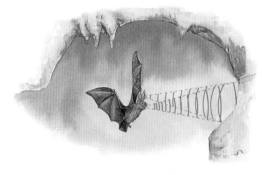

Figure 6.1 *A bat using echolocation in a cave.*

Using echoes

How can you locate something at the bottom of the sea or find out how deep the sea is? You can use echoes. Imagine you are looking for a shipwreck at the bottom of the sea. The ship you are on sends out a sound signal and receives the echo 1 s later. Sound travels at 1500 m/s in water. How deep is the wreck at this point?

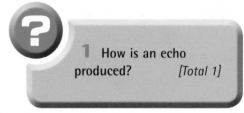

? **1** How is an echo produced? [Total 1]

0.5s for signal to get from wreck to ship

0.5s for signal to get from wreck to ship

Figure 6.2

2 How deep would the wreck have been in the example opposite if the ship were on a freshwater lake? The speed of sound in freshwater is 1400 m/s.

[Total 2]

Example
It takes the signal 1 s to go to the wreck and back. It will take 0.5 s to travel one way.
Sound travels at 1500 m/s in water. In 0.5 s it will travel:
distance = speed × time
= 1500 m/s × 0.5 s
= 750 m
The wreck is 750 m below the ship.

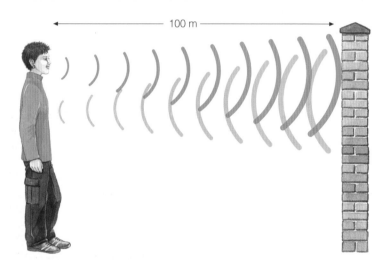

Working out the speed of sound

It is possible to measure the speed of sound using echoes. To do the experiment stand a measured distance away from a tall building or wall. Try to make the distance more than 50 m. Clap your hands once and listen for an echo. As soon as you hear the echo clap again. Ask your partner to time 10 claps. Remember to clap as soon as you hear the echo.

Figure 6.3 *Experiment to work out the speed of sound.*

Example
Harry and Megan carried out the experiment. Harry stood 100 m from the wall. Megan timed 10 claps over 6 s.

The sound has travelled 100 m × 2 for one journey.
Harry clapped 10 times. Therefore the sound travelled 100 × 2 × 10 in 6 seconds = 2000 m.

To work out the speed, the distance travelled by the sound needs to be divided by the time taken. So in 1s it has travelled 2000 ÷ 6 = 333 m/s.

Ultrasound

A sound wave that is too high pitched for humans to hear is called **ultrasound** and is above about 20 kHz (1 kHz is 1000 Hz). The beams of sound reflect from organs in the body and can be used like X-rays. They do not damage tissue like X-rays do. Ultrasound can be used to look at a fetus in the womb without the risk of harm to the unborn baby. If a narrow beam of sound is used then a detailed image is produced.

Sound at this frequency can also make small particles vibrate and can be used to clean delicate and valuable fabrics, glass, spectacles and even teeth.

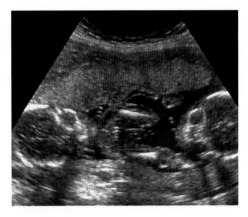

Figure 6.4 *An ultrasound image of twin fetuses.*

Summary

- ○ The reflection of sound is an echo.
- ○ A sound too high to hear with the human ear is called ultrasound.
- ○ Ultrasound can be used to detect objects under the sea, to clean objects and to monitor babies in the womb.

Questions

1 Astronauts who visited the moon put a mirror on its surface. Pulses of light can be used to measure the distance between the Earth and the Moon. Why cannot sound waves be used to do this? *[Total 2]*

2 If you were on the Moon you would not be able to talk to anyone without using a radio.
a) Can you devise a way to speak to someone? *[2]*
b) Briefly describe how your idea would work. *[2]*
[Total 4]

3 Why can't you hear a dog whistle when it is blown?
[Total 2]

4 Using a sound signal, a fisherman finds a shoal of fish under his boat. It took 4 s for the signal to go to the fish and back. If sound travels in water at 1500 m/s how far under the boat are the fish? Show how you worked out the answer.
[Total 3]

5 Your room echoes when you speak. What could you do to your room to try to prevent the echoes?
[Total 3]

6 Why is ultrasound monitoring of fetuses similar to mapping the seabed? *[Total 2]*

Uses and dangers of light and sound

! Dolphins 'see' using echolocation. This allows them produce ultrasound pictures in their minds of the underwater environment.

Using sound

It was during the First World War that submarines first threatened shipping. The submarines could travel under water undetected, but the French scientist Paul Langevin (1872–1946) had an idea.

Figure 7.1 *Submarines in harbour.*

Langevin studied with Pierre Curie (1859–1906), who had discovered a way of generating ultrasound. Langevin realised that ultrasound could travel in a beam through water and be reflected off submerged objects. By detecting the echoes, the position of the objects could be found. His invention, **sonar** or echolocation, came too late to help in the First World War but became very important in the Second World War when German U-boats attempted to destroy convoys of Allied ships.

Today, pregnant women have ultrasound scans to get a picture of their unborn babies. It was Scottish doctor, Ian Donald (1910–1987) who started scanning fetuses in the womb. In 1939, he joined the RAF and became fascinated by gadgets. In the 1950s, he combined his medical knowledge with his technical skills to develop ultrasonic scans on women in Glasgow.

? **1** Why were ultrasound scans on women not done before the First World War?
[Total 2]

Invisible light?

The colours of the rainbow that we can see are known as **visible light**. When the frequency of light waves goes above or below these limits, our eyes cannot detect the light. Violet has the highest frequency of visible light. Frequencies higher than this give **ultra-violet (UV)** light, which we cannot see, and even higher frequencies give **X-rays** and **gamma rays. Infra-red (IR)** light is below the frequency that humans can detect. At even lower frequencies are **microwaves** and **radio** waves. All of these different frequencies of light – visible and invisible – are types of **electromagnetic (EM)** waves. They all travel at the speed of light.

Uses and dangers of light and sound 2

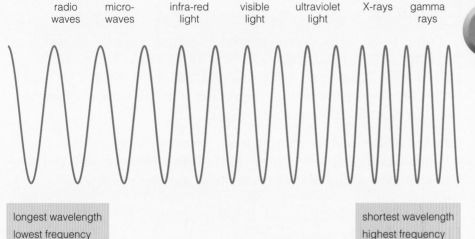

Figure 7.2 *The electromagnetic spectrum – it is like an extended version of the rainbow which includes all the colours that we cannot see.*

? 2 Name three different parts of the electromagnetic spectrum.

[Total 3]

3 How are radio waves and microwaves different?

[Total 2]

4 List the parts of the electromagnetic spectrum in order from highest frequency to lowest frequency

[Total 5]

Communication

You will be familiar with the use of radio waves in broadcast communications. Radio is used all over the world. Terrestrial TV stations in the UK are also broadcast using radio waves. There are so many radio transmissions on Earth that our planet is completely awash with these waves. It is fortunate that there are no known health hazards from them.

With a slightly shorter wavelength than radio waves, microwaves are also used widely in communications. Mobile telephones transmit and receive using these, and they are particularly important in communications with satellites. There has been some argument amongst scientists about whether microwaves pose any risks to our health. At present, it is thought that the energy levels used in mobile phones are not dangerous. However, the World Health Organisation (WHO) recommends that governments do not give out advice on the use of mobile phones until research provides scientists with evidence about their dangers.

Infra-red can also be used in communications as the waves can be carried by an optical fibre like that in an endoscope. The infra-red can be transmitted in pulses to form a coded signal in the fibre. This is the system used for cable TV and broadband internet connections.

Figure 7.3 *Radio and microwaves are used for communications.*

! Fibre optics carrying broadband communications is a new innovation. Previously, computers transmitted information through sounds sent along a phone line. This was a far slower way to transmit data. And there was no internet at all before 1990. Try to imagine a world without it!

5 Why would it be dangerous to remove the door on your microwave oven and keep it working?

[Total 1]

!

Birds and bees can see ultra-violet light. Some bats and snakes can see infra-red light.

Cooking

Our other main use of microwaves is in cooking. Microwaves with a frequency of 2.45 billion hertz can heat up water and fat molecules. This could be dangerous to us as it could heat the water and fat in our bodies. Microwave ovens have metal cases to block these microwaves and stop them from reaching us.

Infra-red is also used for cooking food. For example, in a toaster infra-red waves carry heat directly to the bread. However, this can also lead to danger, as the heat can easily burn us.

Uses of ultra-violet

As the frequency of EM waves increases, they have more energy. This part of the electromagnetic spectrum, with a higher frequency than visible light, interacts with human skin to cause it to tan, so sunbeds have bulbs emitting ultra-violet light. Too much exposure, giving the skin large doses of energy, can lead to skin cancer.

Some chemicals will fluoresce (glow) when they are illuminated with ultra-violet light. This can be used for security markings as the chemicals are invisible in normal light.

Figure 7.4 *Infra-red rays are also often called 'heat radiation'.*

Figure 7.5 *How a bird sees a flower using the ultra-violet part of the EM spectrum compared with how we see it using visible light.*

Medical uses of waves

X-rays can be used for scans which show up solid objects inside an opaque container. A luggage scanner at an airport can show up a gun inside a suitcase, or an X-ray scan of a medical patient can show the bones inside the body without the need to cut the patient open. As they have very high frequencies, the energy levels for X-rays make them quite dangerous. X-ray exposure can lead to cancer, so care must be taken not to scan a patient too often. People who work with X-rays, like dentists, must ensure that they protect themselves against exposure. This is usually done by moving out of the room or behind a lead shield when the X-ray machine is operating.

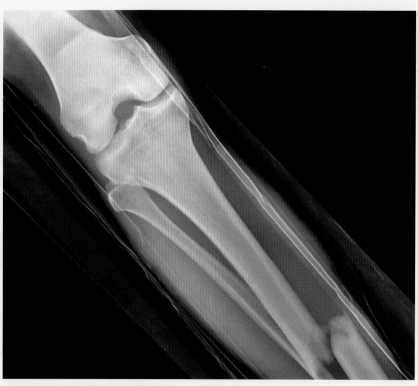

Figure 7.6 *An X-ray scan.*

The very highest frequency electromagnetic waves are gamma rays. These have so much energy that they are very hazardous to human health. They can kill cells directly, and even low levels of exposure can lead to cancer in the longer term. Gamma rays can be used for sterilization of fresh fruit, or of surgical instruments, by killing any bacteria cells. Carefully directed, they are used in hospital radiotherapy treatments to kill cancer cells.

Questions

1 Pick one part of the electromagnetic spectrum and describe a use for it. Include any hazards it poses to health and how we can protect against them.
[Total 3]

2 Why might it be easier for a bird to fly safely through a dark wood than for you to run safely through it?
[Total 2]

3 How is seeing with visible light different from a bat's echolocation system? (Other than using light instead of sound!)
[Total 1]

4 Mobile phone microwaves pose no risk to health. Why then must an engineer working on a mobile phone mast transmitter make sure it is switched off in order to be safe?
[Total 2]

2 Light and sound

Different types of telescope

Looking at the sky

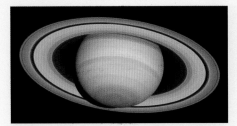

Figure 7.7 *A photo of Saturn from the Hubble Space Telescope.*

When it was first launched, in 1990, the Hubble Space Telescope primary mirror was incorrectly manufactured. A space shuttle repair mission was sent up in 1993, and added a sequence of correcting mirrors to overcome the problem.

The telescope was probably invented in Holland late in the sixteenth century but it was Galileo Galilei (1564–1642) who turned it into a useful instrument. He ground the lenses of his telescope with care and positioned them in a long tube. He found that when he looked into the sky he could see things that nobody had seen before. He observed that the Moon has mountains, that Jupiter has its own moons and that the Sun has spots. Other people copied Galileo's designs and their astronomical discoveries helped to convince most people that the Earth and the planets orbit the Sun.

More powerful telescopes need bigger lenses, but big lenses can produce distorted images. Isaac Newton (1642–1727) designed a telescope that used curved mirrors – a reflecting telescope. This kind of telescope could be made very large without distorting the image and could be used to see very distant objects in space. All the major astronomical telescopes today, including the Hubble Space Telescope, are based on Newton's design. The Hubble Space Telescope was put into orbit by the space shuttle in 1990 and orbits the Earth at a height of 610 km. Since its launch it has taken many pictures of stars, many of which had never been seen before.

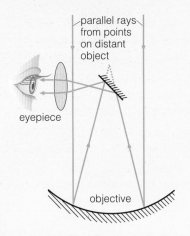

Figure 7.8 *How a reflecting telescope works.*

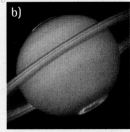

1 Why did Newton design his telescope using mirrors instead of lenses?

Total *[3]*

Astronomy across the spectrum

Stars give out energy in the form of electromagnetic (EM) waves. This means that we can see the visible light that comes from them but that they actually emit waves right across the EM spectrum. People have designed devices to detect each type of electromagnetic wave, and so it is now possible for astronomers to look at stars and galaxies in every part of the EM spectrum. Indeed, the Hubble Space Telescope can detect infra-red, visible light and ultra-violet radiation.

Figure 7.9 *The Hubble Space Telescope can take pictures in ultra-violet, infra-red or visible light (Figure 7.7). Here Saturn is viewed in a) ultra-violet and b) infra-red.*

Radio astronomy

As a very rough rule of thumb, a detector of electromagnetic radiation needs to be about the size as the wavelength of the wave to be effective. The light sensitive cells in your retina are similar to the size of the wavelengths of light that they can detect. So to detect the radio or microwave emissions from stars, we need to use much bigger detectors, as these wavelengths can range from one millimetre to several metres. This is why radio telescopes are such large dish shapes. Indeed, some radio telescopes work together so that the size of the detector is as large as the distance between them, which may be many kilometres.

> **!** Radio wavelengths over ten metres cannot penetrate our atmosphere.

> **?** **2** Why are radio telescopes much larger than visible light telescopes?
> *Total [1]*

Figure 7.10 *The Very Large Array (VLA) radio telescope in New Mexico has twenty-seven, 230 ton, 25 metre diameter radio dishes that work together.*

X-ray and gamma ray astronomy

X-rays and gamma rays are also emitted by stars, but very few penetrate our atmosphere. This means that these areas of astronomy have only developed in the last 50 years since we could put detectors onto high altitude balloons, or on satellites in orbit around Earth.

> **!** Black holes and neutron stars do not emit visible light so cannot be detected using light telescopes. We therefore have to detect them using their emissions in other parts of the EM spectrum, such as the X-rays given off from material as it accelerates into a black hole.

Questions

1 Why have X-ray and gamma ray astronomy only developed in the last 50 years, whilst visible light telescopes have been in use for centuries? *[Total 2]*

2 Pick one part of the electromagnetic spectrum and describe how astronomy can be carried out using that part. *[Total 3]*

3 a) Suggest what problems there are with telescopes on the ground, that are not present for telescopes mounted on satellites. *[2]*

b) Suggest what difficulties there are with telescopes on satellites, that are not present for telescopes on the ground. *[2]*
[Total 4]

End of section questions

1 You want to know the time and you look through the window at a clock. The hands are pointing to 3.15. This does not seem right to you and then you realise you were looking at a reflection of the clock in a mirror. What is the real time? *[Total 2]*

2 a) A director was concerned about the effect of coloured lights on his stage set. He had some green trees on stage and for one scene he wanted them to appear black. What colour lights must he use? *[2]*

 b) He also wanted a background that would change colour with the light, what colour should this be and why? *[2]*
 [Total 4]

3 The time keeper for a 100 m race is standing at the finish line. The starting pistol is fired. How long will it take the sound to reach the timekeeper. (The speed of sound in air is 330 m/s.) *[Total 3]*

4 a) Kyle was watching a football match and his team were wearing yellow shirts with a white collar and red stripes. The floodlights were turned on but someone had changed the bulbs and the light was red. What effect would this have on the colour of the football strip? *[2]*

 b) The opposing team were wearing white shirts and black shorts. How did the appearance of their strip change? *[2]*

 c) Why is it important to have daylight bulbs in the floodlights? *[2]*
 [Total 6]

5 Ben was watching a storm from his house and using his watch he found that there were five seconds between seeing a flash of light and hearing the thunder.

 a) Why did Ben see the lightning before hearing the thunder? *[1]*

 b) How far away is the storm? (The speed of sound in air is 330 m/s) *[2]*

 c) The storm came closer to the house.
 i) What difference if any would Ben notice in the amplitude of the sound wave?
 ii) What would happen to the gap between seeing the lightning flash and hearing the thunder? *[4]*
 [Total 7]

6 a) A sound wave in a fresh water lake takes 4 s to return to the surface of the lake. How deep is the lake at that point? *[2]*

 b) If the same readings were taken in the sea would you expect the sea to be slightly more or less deep? (The speed of sound in fresh water is 1400 m/s; the speed of sound in salt water is 1500 m/s.) *[2]*
 [Total 4]

7 A student collected some data about hearing ranges from different age groups. There were 100 people in each group.
 In the under 10 year age group 80% of the people tested could hear the complete range from 20 Hz to 20 000 Hz. 10% of the remaining sample could not hear the low notes. The rest could not hear the high notes.
 In the 10 to 40 year age group 40% of the people tested could hear all the range. From the remaining sample 20 people could not hear the high notes and the rest could not hear the low notes.
 In the over 40 year age group only 10 people could hear all the range. 80% of the rest could not hear the high or low notes.

 a) Sort out the data so that it is easier to use. You can use charts tables or graphs. *[2]*

 b) Write a short paragraph linking hearing range to age. *[2]*

c) Suggest ways in which you could make the
   results more reliable. *[2]*
   [Total 6]

8 Letitia has dropped a coin behind her wardrobe. It is
on the floor at the back in a very dark corner. She
can reach it but she cannot see it. In her room she
has a ceiling light and a mirror. Draw a plan of how
she could use these to see the coin. *[Total 4]*

9 a) Ultrasound can be used to clean antique fabrics
   and delicate artefacts. What are the advantages
   of using ultrasound instead of water? *[2]*
   b) Ultrasound can also be used for cleaning teeth.
   What are the advantages here? *[2]*
   [Total 4]

10 The bubbles of air rising from a fish are round in
shape. Copy and complete the ray diagram
(Figure 1) to show what happens to the light rays
going through a bubble. *[Total 3]*

11 P Find out how different coloured writing can
affect a person's ability to read words.

12 P Your classroom needs soundproofing. Investigate
the best way to do this.

13 R Our sky looks blue and sunsets are reddish. What
causes these phenomena? Can you explain them
in terms of white light and the spectrum?

14 R How do rock musicians protect their ears from
noise-related damage?

15 R Musical instruments produce sound in different
ways. Find out how a flute, sitar and piano
produce their sounds.

16 R When a pregnant woman is given an ultrasound
scan a narrow beam is used. Find out why this is
better than a wide beam.

Figure 1

3.1 The Universe

Where did the **Universe** begin? What is a comet? Are there such things as shooting stars?

Figure 1.1 *This computer artwork shows how a galaxy may have formed after the 'Big Bang'.*

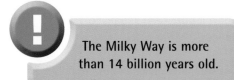

The Milky Way is more than 14 billion years old.

It is possible that all matter started as a tiny, dense, hot mass, which exploded and is gradually expanding. This explosion is called the **'big bang'**. Measurements made by the astronomer Edwin Hubble in the 1920s gave us the first indication that the Universe is expanding. If an object is moving away from us, its light is distorted giving a redder colouring. This is called the red shift. Hubble realised that galaxies furthest away from us have the biggest red shift and so are moving fastest.

It could have started from the collapse of a previous universe. Perhaps in hundreds of billions of years time our Universe will collapse and a new one begin. Billions of years ago, clouds of matter (any substance with mass) came together to form galaxies and within each **galaxy** stars began to form. There are billions of galaxies and each contains billions of stars.

The Milky Way is our galaxy and the Sun is on the edge of this galaxy. The Sun is one of billions of stars which make up the Milky Way.

Most of the stars you can see in the sky are part of the Milky Way galaxy. When you look at the stars you are looking into history, because light from them takes hundreds, or even thousands, of years to reach the Earth. The light from a star reaching Earth tonight could have left

Figure 1.2 *The Milky Way.*

the star before dinosaurs were on Earth. This is because light travelling at 300 000 000 m/s takes this long to cover such vast distances.

Our knowledge of space originally came from observing the sky with the naked eye. Telescopes were first used to look at the planets and the stars in the seventeenth century. As time passed bigger and better telescopes were developed. These gave people a more detailed view of space. However, dust and water vapour in the Earth's atmosphere make it difficult to see details of the planets, or to observe distant, faint stars. Modern telescopes are built on mountain tops, so they are above the clouds. The best views of space are obtained from the Hubble Space Telescope, which orbits the Earth in space.

We have obtained more information about the planets in our solar system by sending unmanned probes to the planets. Space probes have flown close to all the planets, and some have landed on Venus and Mars. In 1990 *Voyager 1* photographed the solar system from the edge of the system. There have been many probes sent to investigate different planets, including the *Galileo* probe which gathered information on Jupiter and its moons from 1995 to 2003. The *Cassini* probe is gathering data about Saturn and its moons, and sent the Huygens probe to investigate the atmosphere of Titan, Saturn's largest moon. Several landers and rovers have been sent to Mars.

The Sun

The Sun is a star. If you were standing a long way out in space and looking at the Sun it would be a small, not very bright, star.

The Sun does not burn like a fire. Inside the Sun hydrogen atoms join together to produce helium atoms. This is called **nuclear fusion**. When this reaction happens a lot of energy is released. This is the energy that gives the Earth heat and light. The Sun is a middle-aged star; it is half-way through its life. There is enough hydrogen left to give out energy for another 5000 million years.

Eventually the Sun, like other small stars, will collapse in on itself and become a **white dwarf**. When stars much bigger than the Sun collapse they create a large gravitational pull. Nothing, not even light, can escape from the pull of the gravitational field. This is called a **black hole**.

The Sun and the **planets** were formed from a swirling cloud of dust and gas. Part of the cloud formed the Sun, and other small clumps of matter joined together to form the planets.

! The only humans to visit other bodies in the solar system were 12 Apollo astronauts, who visited the Moon between 1969 and 1972.

? 1 Why are the best images of space obtained from a space telescope?
[Total 1]

! *Voyager 1* is the furthest human-made object from Earth. In 2009 it was over 16 billion km from Earth and still going!

(not to scale)
asteroids
Haumea
Makemake
Eris
Pluto
Sun
Mars
Earth
Uranus
Venus
Mercury
Ceres
Jupiter
Saturn
Neptune

Figure 1.3 *The solar system.*

> **!**
>
> To remember the order of the planets, use this phrase. <u>M</u>y <u>V</u>ery <u>E</u>xcellent <u>M</u>other <u>J</u>ust <u>S</u>ent <u>Us</u> <u>N</u>achos. Or you could make up one of your own.

The Sun is the centre of our **solar system** with eight planets in orbit around it. The planets are held in their orbits by the Sun's gravity. Planets do not give off light like the Sun. The planets can be seen because they are illuminated by the Sun and reflect the Sun's light. The orbits of the planets are **elliptical** (oval).

The planets

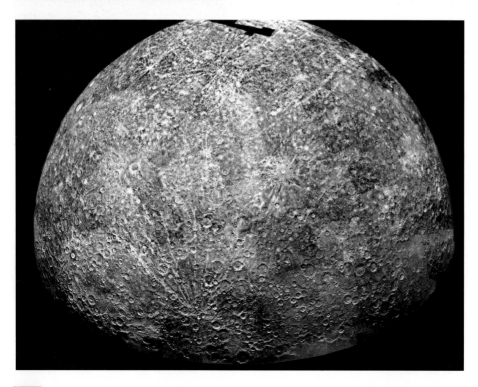

Mercury

Mercury is the closest planet to the Sun and is very hot. It has a surface temperature of over 400 °C on the daylight side and –180 °C on the night side. Mercury has the shortest year because it is the closest planet to the Sun. Mercury is covered in craters and has no atmosphere.

Figure 1.4 *Mercury.*

Figure 1.5 *An image of Venus made using radar information.*

Venus

Venus is the hottest planet because the carbon dioxide in its atmosphere creates a greenhouse effect and helps to hold in heat energy. Clouds of sulphuric acid surround Venus. This makes it very difficult to land a spacecraft on it.

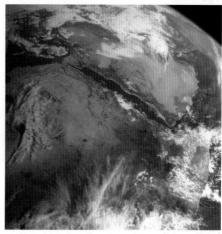

Figure 1.6 *Earth.*

Earth

Earth is the only planet which can support our life form because the temperature on the Earth's surface is not too hot or cold. It has liquid water on the surface and clouds of water vapour swirling round it.

Mars

Mars is a rocky mountainous planet that looks red and is often called the red planet. The very thin atmosphere is mainly carbon dioxide. Several space probes have landed on Mars to sample the surface. They have found evidence that there was once liquid water on Mars.

Figure 1.7 *The surface of Mars.*

Jupiter

Jupiter is the largest planet in our solar system. It is almost twice as large as all the other planets put together. The planet is made up mainly of hydrogen and helium. There is a huge hurricane-like 'storm' called the red spot. The storm is almost three times the size of Earth. Jupiter has a ring around it made of rock and ice crystals. The largest of Jupiter's moons, Ganymede, is rocky and about half the size of the Earth.

Figure 1.8 *Jupiter.*

Saturn

Saturn, like Jupiter, is made mainly of hydrogen and helium. It has a large set of rings around it made of rock and ice crystals. Saturn is the least dense of all the planets.

Figure 1.9 *Saturn.*

Uranus

Uranus was discovered in 1781 by William Herschel. Little was known about the planet until 1986 when *Voyager 2* passed close to it. It has many rings made from rock and ice. Although it is smaller than Saturn and Jupiter, it is still sixty times as large as Earth. It has an atmosphere of hydrogen, helium and methane.

Figure 1.10 *Uranus.*

Neptune

Neptune was not discovered until 1846 because it is so far away from the Earth and difficult to see with telescopes. Neptune has rings and a blue methane atmosphere. Neptune has the fiercest winds in the solar system. It has large dark spots and fast moving white clouds. *Voyager* scientists called one large white cloud Scooter because it 'scoots' round the planet.

Data on the planets are shown in Table 1.1.

Dwarf planets

Until 2006, astronomers said that the solar system had nine planets. However some people thought that Pluto was too small to be a planet. In 2005 a new body was discovered orbiting far beyond Pluto. It was also bigger than Pluto. If Pluto is a planet, then this new body, Eris, should also be called a planet.

In 2006, astronomers at a meeting of the International Astronomical Union decided that to be a planet, bodies had to:

- be big enough for their gravity to have made them become spherical

- have 'cleared their orbit' of other rocks and debris by colliding with them or disrupting their orbits.

Pluto has not 'cleared its orbit', so it was put into the **dwarf planet** category, together with Eris, Ceres, and two other bodies orbiting well beyond Pluto. The region just beyond Pluto's orbit is called the Kuiper Belt, and astronomers expect to find more dwarf planets and smaller bodies there.

Asteroids

The solar system also contains millions of **asteroids**. These are small, rocky bodies, mostly orbiting between the orbits of Mars and Jupiter. Some asteroids have orbits that take them close to the Earth, and it is possible than an asteroid will collide with the Earth.

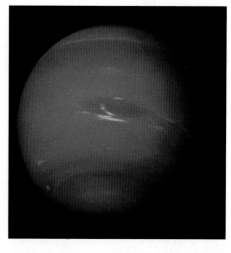

Figure 1.11 *Neptune.*

2 List the five dwarf planets (see Figure 1.3).
[Total 2]

Many scientists think that an asteroid or comet hitting the Earth was the cause of the dinosaurs becoming extinct.

Table 1.1

Planet	Mean surface temperature (°C)	Time to spin once	Time to orbit Sun (Earth days)
Mercury	350 to –170	58.6 days	88 days
Venus	465	243 days	225 days
Earth	15	24 h	365.25 days
Mars	–46	24 h 37 min	687 days
Jupiter	–108	9 h 56 min	11.9 years
Saturn	–139	10 h 35 min	29.7 years
Uranus	–197	1h 14 min	84 years
Neptune	–201	1h 6 min	165 years

Planet	Surface gravity relative to Earth*	Density (kg/m^3)	Mass relative to Earth**	Moons
Mercury	0.38	5400	0.06	0
Venus	0.90	5200	0.82	0
Earth	1	5500	1	1
Mars	0.38	3900	0.11	2
Jupiter	2.5	1300	318	63+
Saturn	0.9	700	95	34+
Uranus	0.9	1300	14.5	21+
Neptune	1.1	1600	17.1	13+

*The 'gas giants' (Jupiter, Saturn, Uranus and Neptune) do not have solid surfaces. The 'surface' referred to here is the level where the gas pressure is equal to atmospheric pressure on Earth.
**Mass of Earth = 5.9 thousand billion billion tonnes.

Meteors and comets

Meteors

Meteoroids are small pieces of asteroids or comets, and are not normally visible in the sky. At certain times in the year the Earth passes through the debris left by comets, and **meteor showers** can be seen. If they enter the Earth's atmosphere the heat energy produced by friction with the atmosphere makes them glow. They are called **meteors** or **'shooting stars'**. Some meteors could be debris from spacecraft. This debris burns up in the Earth's atmosphere. Any meteor that is large enough to travel through the atmosphere and hit the Earth is called a **meteorite**. There is no record of anyone being killed by a meteorite. However, meteorites have hit the Earth and made huge craters.

The craters made on Earth by meteorite impacts are very similar to the ones on the Moon. The Moon has no atmosphere to destroy the craters, so they main remain visible on the Moon for a long time. Some meteors are metallic, some are made of stone and a few are crumbly rock.

Comets

Comets are lumps of ice and dust orbiting the Sun in very elongated orbits. Comets were formed at the same time as our solar system.

As the comet gets closer to the Sun its surface starts to melt and gives off clouds of dust and gas. The tail of a comet is this dust and gas lit up by the Sun. The tail always faces away from the Sun. As the comet travels further away from the Sun it re-freezes and the tail disappears.

Figure 1.13 *Meteorite crater, Arizona.*

?

3 "The same piece of rock can be a meteoroid, a meteor and a meteorite." Explain this statement.

[Total 3]

4 Write down two differences between a comet and a meteoroid.

[Total 2]

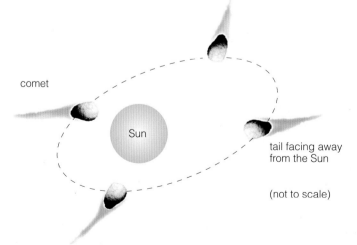

comet

Sun

tail facing away from the Sun

(not to scale)

Figure 1.14 *The orbit of a comet.*

Comets are usually named after the people who discovered them. Halley's comet was named after Edmund Halley, an English scientist. It was first seen in China in 240BCE, but it was Halley who first noticed that it returned regularly. The comet returns close to the Earth every 76 years and was last seen in 1986.

Summary

- The Sun is one star out of billions in the Milky Way galaxy.
- The Sun is the centre of the solar system.
- Nuclear fusion provides the Sun's energy.
- The solar system is made up of the Sun, eight orbiting planets, five dwarf planets, comets and asteroids.
- Only Earth has an atmosphere that will support our life form.
- Meteors are small pieces of rock that sometimes fall to Earth.

Questions

1 Copy and complete these sentences.
There are _____ planets in the solar system. These planets are held in orbit around the _____ by the Sun's _____. The hottest planet is _____, because the gases in its atmosphere cause a _____ effect. The largest planet is _____. The planet nearest to the Sun is _____. Four planets have rings; these are Jupiter, Saturn, _____ and _____. A planet does not travel in a circular orbit around the Sun but in an _____.
[Total 5]

2 'My Very Excellent Mother Just Sent Us Nougat' is one way of remembering the order of the planets from the Sun. Work out a sentence of your own to help you remember this order. [Total 2]

3 a) List the similarities and differences between planets and dwarf planets. [3]
b) When this book was written there were five dwarf planets. Explain why this number may increase. [2]
[Total 5]

4 Choose one of the planets in the solar system. Write an advertisement or travel brochure to encourage people to visit the planet. Try to include information about temperature, day length, atmosphere and gravity. [Total 4]

5 Planets do not give off their own light and yet we can see them. Explain why. [Total 2]

6 How is a planet's distance from the Sun related to the length of its year? [Total 3]

3.2 Earth

What causes day and night? Does the Moon have any effect on the Earth? There are parts of the Earth where it is dark for 24 hours or more. This is caused by seasonal changes and depends on where you are on the Earth.

The Earth spins on its axis and takes 24 hours to complete one rotation. This gives us our days and nights.

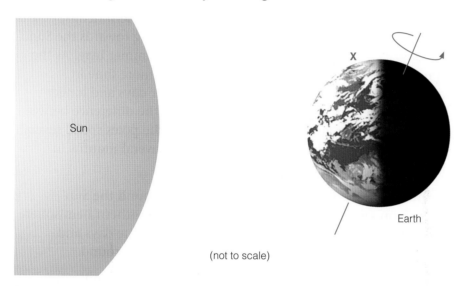

Sun

Earth

(not to scale)

Figure 2.1 *Day and night.*

As the Earth spins, to someone standing at point X on Figure 2.1, the Sun appears to move across the sky. However, it is really the Earth that is moving, not the Sun. Twenty-four hours later point X will be back where it started. We say that the Sun rises in the east and sets in the west. This is because of the way the Earth rotates. To a person at point X, as the Earth spins the Sun appears on the eastern horizon. The person moves past the Sun until the Sun goes behind the western horizon. The same thing appears to happen with the stars – as the Earth rotates they seem to move across the sky.

Day and night

When point X on Figure 2.1 is pointing towards the Sun the area will be in daylight. As the Earth rotates this area will gradually change to darkness or night time. It takes 24 hours for the Earth to make one revolution, but day time and night time are not each 12 hours long unless you are on the Equator. The length of day and night depend on where you live on the Earth, and what time of year it is.

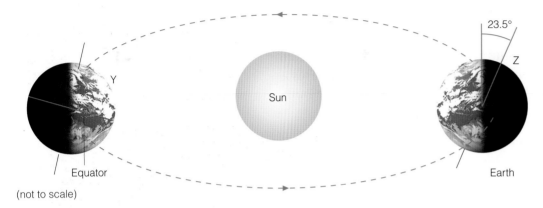

Figure 2.2 *The Earth's orbit around the Sun.*

The Earth's axis is tilted at an angle of 23.5°, which means that day length and seasons change, according to where the Earth is in its orbit around the Sun.

When the Earth is at position Y on Figure 2.2, the northern hemisphere is pointing towards the Sun. It is summer here. As the Earth rotates, the southern hemisphere will spend more time in darkness. It is winter here. This would mean colder days and longer nights. As you get further away from the Equator the difference between day and night length gets bigger. Countries near the poles spend several months of the year in almost total darkness and several months in continuous daylight.

Six months later the Earth has travelled half-way round the Sun (position Z on Figure 2.2). Now it is winter in the northern hemisphere and here the days will be very short. At the Equator the days and nights remain at twelve hours each, as they do all year round.

The Equator is the hottest part of the world because the Sun's energy is more concentrated here. The same energy reaches all parts of the Earth. Because the Earth is curved the energy is less concentrated as

> **!** The Earth is slightly closer to the Sun when it is winter in the UK than it is in the summer.

> **?** **1** List three differences between summer and winter. [Total 3]

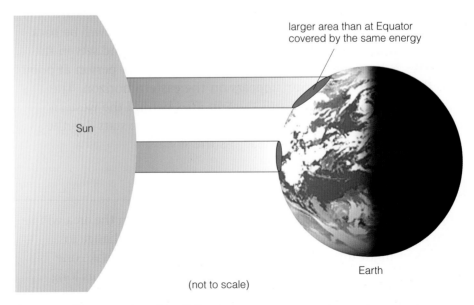

Figure 2.3 *Concentration of sunlight.*

you move away from the Equator, as it is spread over a larger area. This also contributes to seasonal temperature variations.

It takes the Earth $365\frac{1}{4}$ days to orbit the Sun. It is not possible to have one-quarter of a day so every four years these are added together to give an extra day at the end of February which is called a **leap day**. When there is a leap day in the year, the year is a called a **leap year**.

The Moon

The Moon is a **natural satellite** orbiting the Earth. It takes 29.5 days or one 'moonth' to go around the Earth. The Moon rotates much more slowly than the Earth. It completes one rotation in the time it takes to orbit the Earth once. This means that the same side of the Moon always faces the Earth.

The gravitational pull of the Moon on the Earth causes the tides.

Phases of the Moon

The Moon is illuminated by the Sun and reflects the light of the Sun towards the Earth. When the Moon is between the Sun and the Earth the side of the Moon lit by the Sun cannot be seen from Earth. It is a new moon. As the Moon orbits the Earth more of the lit side of the Moon becomes visible. The Moon can be seen as a crescent moon, half moon and eventually a full moon as the sunlit side faces Earth. The process reverses as the Moon continues to orbit the Earth. After about 29.5 days the lit side of the Moon is invisible again. It is back to a new moon.

Eclipse of the Moon

Sometimes the Moon goes through the Earth's shadow. The Moon is not invisible because a small amount of diffuse light will reach it. A **lunar eclipse** does not happen every month because the orbit of the Moon is tilted compared with the orbit of the Earth. This means that the Moon does not go through the Earth's shadow every month.

> **!** The word lunatic (moonstruck) meant a person affected by the Moon.

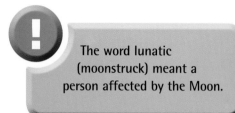

Sun

new moon

Earth

full moon

(not to scale)

Figure 2.4 *Phases of the Moon.*

> **!** Until spacecraft orbited the Moon, no-one had seen what the back of the Moon looked like as it cannot be seen from the Earth.

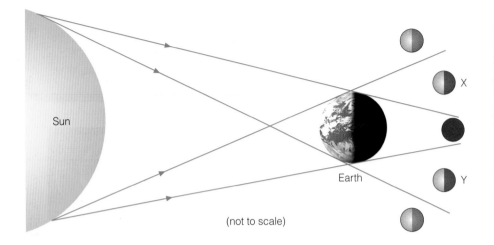

Figure 2.5 *Eclipse of the Moon. The Moon is only partly shadowed by the Earth at points X and Y.*

?

2 Which kind of eclipse happens at a
a) new moon   [1]
b) full moon?   [1]
          [Total 2]

Eclipse of the Sun

An eclipse of the Sun is a rare event in the UK, and happens when the Moon is between the Sun and the Earth and blocks the Sun's rays. The Earth is rotating and the Moon is orbiting the Earth so a **solar eclipse** does not last for very long. However, there are usually two eclipses of the Sun each year which you can see from somewhere on the Earth.

At position A on Figure 2.6, there will be a total eclipse, with the Sun completely blocked out by the Moon. If you are standing at one of the positions marked B you will see a partial eclipse, where only part of the Sun is blocked out. No eclipse at all will be visible at other places on the Earth.

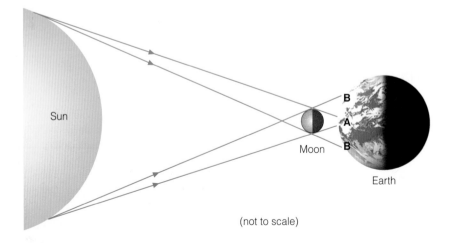

Figure 2.6 *An eclipse of the Sun.*

Figure 2.7 *The Sun in total eclipse.*

Summary

- The Earth spins once on its axis every 24 hours.
- The Earth's axis is tilted at an angle of 23.5°.
- One year is $365\frac{1}{4}$ days, which is the time it takes the Earth to orbit the Sun.
- The Moon is the only natural satellite of Earth and the same side always faces the Earth.
- Phases of the Moon happen because we only see part of the lit side.
- An eclipse of the Moon happens when the Moon goes into the Earth's shadow.
- An eclipse of the Sun occurs when the Moon casts a shadow over part of the Earth.

Questions

1 Copy and complete the following sentences.
In summer the Sun appears _____ in the sky in the middle of the day. When the northern hemisphere is tilted towards the Sun it will be _____ time. There the days will be _____ and the nights _____. The Earth takes _____ hours to spin once and _____ days to orbit the Sun. *[Total 3]*

2 a) Which of the following sentences are correct? *[2]*
  i) The Moon is an artificial satellite.
  ii) The same side of the Moon always faces the Earth.
  iii) An eclipse of the Sun is caused by the shadow of the Earth.
  iv) There are times when the lit side of the Moon faces away from Earth.
  v) An eclipse of the Moon happens more often than an eclipse of the Sun.
 b) For each statement that is incorrect, say what is wrong. Rewrite the statement to make it correct.
  [3]
  [Total 5]

3 Copy Figure 2.8.
 a) Put a cross where it will be summer on Earth. *[1]*
 b) Shade the part of the Earth where it is night. *[1]*
 c) Draw the Earth six months later. *[1]*
 d) Draw the Earth when it is spring in the northern hemisphere. *[1]*
 e) At A there is an eclipse of the Sun. Draw the Moon on the diagram. *[1]*
  [Total 5]

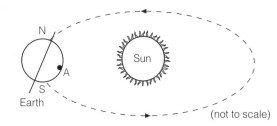

Figure 2.8

4 Explain why is it not correct to say that the Sun rises in the east and sets in the west. *[Total 2]*

3.3 Gravity

Why do you weigh more on the Earth than you do on the Moon? Why do **satellites** not fall down to Earth? We have all gained some understanding of gravity by learning from everyday experiences.

Weight and gravity

An apple hanging from a branch has **mass** and, due to gravity, there is a downward force on it called **weight**. It may become detached from the branch and fall towards the ground.

We tend to think of objects as falling downwards but objects on the other side of the Earth fall in the opposite direction. By saying that objects fall downwards we are really saying that they fall towards the centre of the Earth.

Both the Earth and the apple have mass. **Gravity** causes a force of attraction between the two masses. You can find out more about weight and forces at the start of Section 4.3.

mass

weight

The Earth's gravitational field attracts the apple towards the centre of the Earth.

Earth

Figure 3.1

On Earth a 1 kg mass weighs 10 N

weight (N) = mass (kg) × 10 (N/kg)

Two people standing close to each other both have mass and these two masses will be attracted towards each other by a gravitational force. This attraction will not be noticeable because the mass of a person is insignificant compared to the mass of a planet like the Earth.

Any two particles of matter are attracted to each other. The greater the two masses, the greater the gravitational pull will be. Look at Figure 3.2.

?

1 A box of apples has a mass of 3 kg. How much does the box weigh?

[Total 2]

m   gravitational pull   M

Figure 3.2 *Gravitational force between two masses.*

There is the same gravitation pull on both masses but this will have less effect on the larger mass. For example, a bird flying through the air will be pulled towards the Earth. The Earth will also be pulled towards the bird but, because the Earth has a much greater mass, this will not be noticeable.

Gravity on different planets

On the surface of the Earth a 1.0 kg mass will experience a gravitational force of 10 N and is said to weigh 10 N.

The mass of the Moon is much smaller than the mass of the Earth and therefore the pull of gravity is less. A 1.0 kg mass on the surface of the Moon will weigh about 1.7 N while on the more massive planet of Jupiter it will weigh about 25 N.

A person visiting different planets would have the same mass on each planet but would weigh different amounts according to the planet's gravitational field.

Planets with a stronger gravitational field exert more force on falling objects and therefore objects will accelerate towards the ground at a faster rate.

Travelling away from Earth

As you get further away from the Earth, the influence of gravity decreases. To travel away from the Earth, a rocket needs a force to push against the Earth's gravity.

Rockets like the Space Shuttle have a very large mass. Most of this mass is made up of the fuel storage tanks and the fuel inside them. The fuel is needed to propel the rocket upwards.

At first the rocket accelerates very slowly but as it travels away from the Earth two things happen to help it accelerate faster.

- The gravitational field strength due to the Earth decreases and there is less gravitational force to accelerate against.
- The mass of the rocket decreases as fuel is burnt and fuel tanks are discarded.

Once a spacecraft is in orbit, only short bursts of rocket propulsion are needed to change its speed or direction.

! NASA used the Moon's gravitational field to help change the direction of *Apollo 13* and get it safely back to Earth.

Figure 3.3 *Space Shuttle during launch.*

? **2** Give two reasons why the weight of the Space Shuttle is less when it is in orbit than when it is on the launch pad. *[Total 2]*

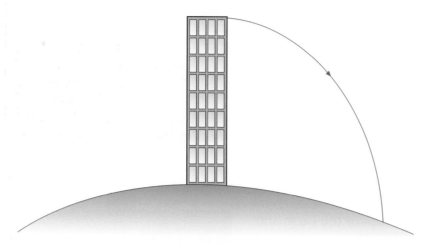

Figure 3.4 *Throwing a stone from a tall building.*

Satellites

Many people believe that satellites orbiting the Earth have escaped from its gravitational field. In fact it is the gravitational force that keeps the satellite in orbit and stops it flying off into space.

It is useful to think about throwing a stone from a very tall building: the stone would follow a curved path until it hit the ground. Figure 3.4 also reminds us that the surface of the Earth is curved.

Now think about firing the stone from a cannon at the top of a tower that was so tall it reached beyond the Earth's atmosphere. If the stone is fired at the right speed it will follow a circular path around the Earth. It is in orbit.

The satellite would continue to travel in a straight line if a force was not acting upon it. The gravitational force from the Earth changes its direction so that it is constantly turning towards the Earth, causing it to follow a circular orbit.

This is very similar to whirling a mass on a string around your head. The force from the string makes the mass go round in a circle. Without this force the mass would fly off and travel in a straight line.

Satellites orbit above the Earth's atmosphere where there is no air resistance to slow them down. At greater heights the gravitational force on a satellite is less and therefore it does not change direction so quickly. The satellite follows a longer path and takes longer to orbit the Earth.

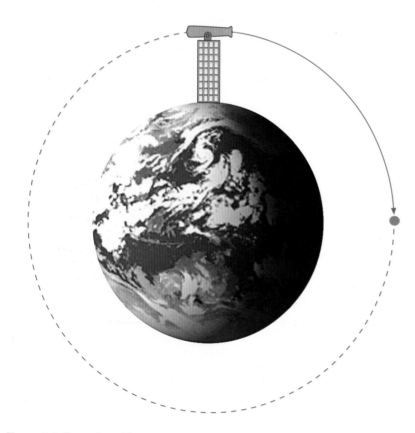

Figure 3.5 *Stone in orbit.*

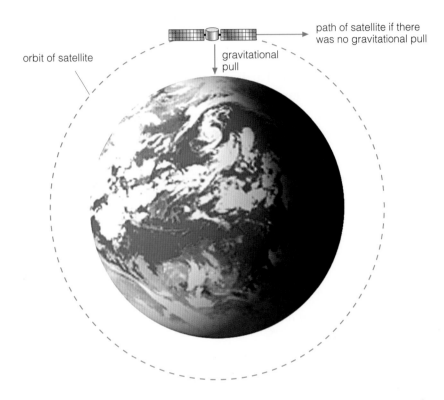

orbit of satellite

path of satellite if there was no gravitational pull

gravitational pull

3 Why doesn't a satelite in orbit need an engine to keep it moving?

[Total 1]

Figure 3.6 *As a satellite orbits the Earth, the surface of the Earth falls away as fast as the satellite falls towards it.*

Geostationary orbit

The time it takes an **artificial satellite** to orbit the Earth can be controlled by choosing the height of its orbit.

Communication satellites such as the ones used for satellite television are in an orbit that takes 24 hours to complete. They are also positioned over the Equator, meaning that they are always above the same point on the Earth as the Earth rotates. This is called a **geostationary** orbit.

If a geostationary orbit were not used people would need to keep changing the direction in which their satellite dishes were pointing.

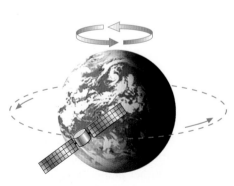

Figure 3.7 *Geostationary orbit.*

The Moon's orbit

The Moon is a lot closer to the Earth than it is to the Sun and it orbits the Earth due to the strong influence of the Earth's gravitational field.

There are a number of theories about how the Moon became a natural satellite in orbit around the Earth. Most scientists think that over 4 billion years ago a very large rock about the size of Mars collided with the Earth. This impact blasted fragments of the Earth into orbit and these fragments then combined to form the Moon.

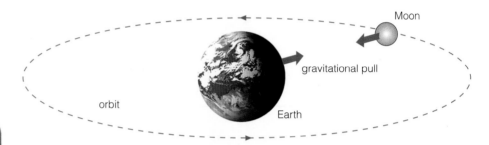

Figure 3.8 *The Moon orbiting the Earth.*

Without the pull from the Earth's gravitational field, the Moon would travel in a straight line and continue out into space.

The average radius of the Moon's orbit is 384 000 km and it takes just under 28 days for the Moon to complete one orbit of the Earth.

Orbiting planets

The planets orbit the Sun in the same way as satellites and the Moon orbit the Earth.

The large gravitational field strength of the Sun provides the forces that keep the planets in their orbits. Planets that are further from the Sun have smaller gravitational pulls acting on them and therefore they take longer to complete one orbit.

Ganymede is one of the four largest moons that orbit the planet Jupiter. Although it is bigger than the planet Mercury it is called a satellite because it orbits a planet and not the Sun.

Summary

- Gravity is the attraction between masses.
- Weight = mass × gravitational field strength.
- The Earth's gravitational field strength = 10 N/kg.
- On Earth, weight (N) = mass (kg) × 10 (N/kg).
- Larger masses have stronger gravitational fields.
- A planet's gravitational field strength decreases with distance from the planet.
- Masses on the surface of the Earth are pulled towards the centre of the Earth.
- The force acting on a mass due to the Earth's gravitational field is called weight.
- Satellites are kept in orbit by the Earth's gravitational pull.
- The Moon is a natural satellite.

Questions

1 The name of the gravitational force acting on a mass on the surface of the Earth is _____. Larger masses have _____ gravitational fields. If the _____ field is stronger on a planet, objects will accelerate towards the ground at a _____ rate. *[Total 2]*

2 Explain why it would require less fuel to launch a rocket from the Moon than it would from the Earth. *[Total 3]*

3 a) What force keeps a satellite in orbit around the Earth? *[1]*

b) Why is it important for satellites to be outside the Earth's atmosphere? *[3]*

[Total 4]

4 Planets closer to the Sun take less time to orbit than those further away. Why is this? *[Total 3]*

5 Table 3.1 shows the weight of a 1.0 kg mass and the weight of a 50.0 kg mass on different planets.

Table 3.1

Planet	Gravitational field strength (N/kg)	Weight of a 1.0 kg mass (N)	Weight of a 50.0 kg mass (N)
Earth	10	10	500
Mercury	4	4	
Jupiter	26		1300
Neptune		12	
Uranus	11		

a) Copy and complete Table 3.1. *[6]*

b) On which one of these five planets would a falling object have the greatest downward acceleration? *[1]*

[Total 7]

Changing ideas

In the past the only information people had about the world came from what they could see. The Earth looked flat and so people thought that you could fall off the end of the Earth. The Greeks were the first people to realise this was not true. They measured the angle of the Sun at two places a known distance apart and worked out the circumference of the Earth. But they thought that the Earth was motionless in space and that the Sun, Moon, planets and the stars all circled around the Earth.

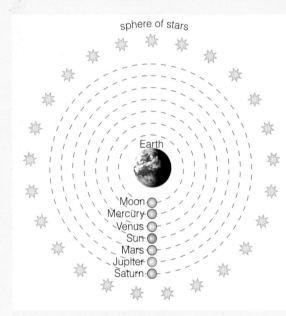

Figure 4.1 *Ptolemy's universe.*

Ptolemy was an Egyptian astronomer who lived in Alexandria, a town founded by the Greeks. He said that the planets went round in small circles called epicycles, while travelling with the Sun and Moon around the Earth. He thought that the stars were points of light fixed on a sphere around the system. The planets were named after Roman gods.

Astronomers observed the planets and were able to use Ptolemy's idea to predict where the planets would be, but the predictions were not always accurate.

A new system

In 1543 Nicolas Copernicus (1473–1543) put forward the view that the Sun was the centre of the solar system and all the planets moved in circles around it. He didn't observe the planets himself, but thought his idea would help astronomers to make more accurate predictions of where the planets would appear in the sky. The Church had adopted Ptolemy's theory, along with other Greek ideas, as being the work of God. God must have put Man on Earth, at the centre of the Universe, and everything above the Earth must be perfect and unchanging. The Church dealt severely with people who had different ideas so Copernicus did not publish his ideas until he was dying.

Tycho Brahe (1546–1601) was a Danish astronomer who made accurate observations of the planets. His observations were made with the naked eye, because telescopes had not been invented. He observed a supernova (an exploding star), which showed that the stars were not permanent and fixed, as the Church thought. But he didn't agree with Copernicus and in his plan of the heavens.

Galileo Galilei (1564–1642) was the first person to use the telescope scientifically. He was the first to discover that other planets had moons and he saw that Venus went through changes like the phases of the

Figure 4.2 *Galileo at work.*

Moon. His observations supported the ideas of Copernicus. Galileo was a respected and well-known lecturer in Florence and he had friends who were high up in the Roman Catholic Church. In 1616, the Church banned Copernicus's book and Galileo was told to stop teaching his ideas about a Sun-centred system.

For a few years Galileo kept quiet but then an old friend became Pope. Galileo was given permission to write a book describing the two views of the Universe. Galileo published his book in 1632 but he had made a mistake. He completely demolished the old ideas and gave all the best arguments to Copernicus. The Pope was furious. He had Galileo arrested, tried for heresy and banned his book. As Galileo was already old he was not tortured or put to death and some friends managed to get his sentence reduced to house arrest. He lived for another ten years writing about his other scientific work. It wasn't until 1992, 350 years later, that the Vatican forgave him for his views.

At the same time that Galileo was studying the sky, Johannes Kepler (1571–1630) was writing three laws describing the ways the planets moved around the Sun. In 1598, he joined Tycho Brahe in Prague. Brahe's observations were accurate enough to help Kepler prove that the planets orbit the Sun. One of the main things he said was that a planet's orbit is elliptical. Kepler's laws are the basis behind our modern understanding of the solar system.

Recent discoveries of more moons of Jupiter and Saturn have been made by space probes. Their pictures and data have given astronomers more information than could ever be obtained using a telescope. The flight paths of the probes proved once again the accuracy of Newton's law of gravitation.

Figure 4.3 *Johannes Kepler.*

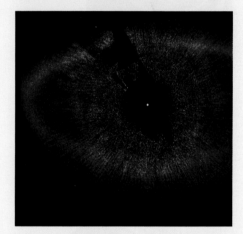

Figure 4.4 *This photo was taken using the Hubble Space Telescope, and shows a planet orbiting a star called Formalhaut.*

Questions

1 How does Ptolemy's view of the known Universe differ from our present view? *[Total 5]*

2 If you watch a ship sail away to the horizon it does not get smaller and smaller, and then disappear – instead it starts to sink below the horizon. How does this information help to explain that the Earth is round and not flat? *[Total 3]*

3 Why do you think the Roman Catholic Church was reluctant to accept Galileo's observations and ideas? *[Total 2]*

4 The white dot in the centre of Figure 4.4 shows the position of Formalhaut, and the black ring around it is where astronomers have masked the image to remove the light coming from the star. Why do you think they needed to do this? *[Total 2]]*

3 Space

Satellites

Figure 4.5 *Sputnik 1.*

The first satellite to be put into orbit around the Earth was *Sputnik 1*, which was launched by USSR in 1957. It was only 58 cm across and orbited the Earth once every 96 minutes. After 57 days in orbit, *Sputnik* burnt up as it re-entered the Earth's atmosphere.

Since then well over 5000 satellites have been launched into orbit around the Earth. Space around the Earth is becoming polluted as many of these satellites are no longer working.

There are various types of satellites which have jobs such as:
- communications
- monitoring weather patterns
- surveying and position finding
- space telescopes.

Polar orbits

A **polar orbit** is used to collect detailed information from around the world, as the satellite's orbit takes it over the North and South Poles as the Earth rotates beneath it. This has the advantage of covering the whole world every day, but the coverage of any one region is not continuous. This also makes transmitting data back to Earth more difficult. The satellite needs to store the data collected and only transmit it to Earth when it is passing over the region where the receiver dish is located.

Figure 4.6 *Polar orbit.*

Weather satellites

Weather satellites are used to study the Earth's weather systems, providing up-to-date information and helping to forecast the weather around the world. To study the weather in only one region a geostationary satellite can be used. It is positioned above the Equator and collects data from the region below. A satellite in geostationary orbit can see one-third of the Earth's surface. If more detailed information is required, a satellite in a polar orbit is used.

Remote surveying and position finding

To take detailed pictures of the Earth's surface, satellites in polar orbits are used as a very high level of detail can be obtained. Spy satellites are in polar orbit.

If you want to find where you are, you can use the Global Positioning System (GPS). This uses over 20 satellites. At any one time, a point on the Earth's surface should be within range of three or four satellites. The positions of these satellites are known very accurately as they are tracked from a ground station. In turn, your position can be worked out to within 5 m or less when the conditions are right.

Communications satellites

Communications satellites are used to carry telephone calls from one side of the Earth to the other and to broadcast television over a large area. These satellites are usually in geostationary orbits. One satellite in geostationary orbit can see one-third of the Earth's surface.

Space Shuttle and International Space Station

The Space Shuttle usually goes into a low-level orbit, up to 480 km above the Earth's surface. The International Space Station is also in this type of orbit. The Space Shuttle will carry new parts of the station into orbit. In these low-level orbits, there is a very small amount of friction from the very thin upper atmosphere. Even though it is very small, it is enough to slow down the satellite so that it will eventually fall back to Earth. The Russian Mir space station fell into the southern Indian Ocean in 2000.

Hubble Space Telescope

The Hubble Space Telescope is in orbit nearly 600 km above the Earth. By being above the Earth's atmosphere, it can take much clearer photographs of objects in the Universe. One camera can take high resolution images which are ten times better than those from the largest telescope on Earth, even though the Hubble Space Telescope is considerably smaller. The faint object camera can detect objects 50 times fainter than anything that can be picked up by a ground-based telescope.

Figure 4.7 *A satellite image of Scotland.*

Figure 4.8 *Hubble Space Telescope being maintained by astronauts from the Space Shuttle*

Questions

1 Draw diagrams to show
   a) a geostationary orbit   [2]
   b) a polar orbit   [2]
   c) a low-level orbit.   [2]
                              [Total 6]

2 Explain why a polar orbit is not suitable for satellite television.   [Total 3]

3 What sort of orbit would you use to obtain detailed pictures of the Earth's surface?   [Total 1]

4 What advantages does a weather satellite in geostationary orbit have over a weather satellite in polar orbit?   [Total 2]

End of section questions

1 Explain why someone might say that a ball dropped in New Zealand will not travel in the same direction as a ball dropped in Scotland.

[Total 2]

2 Why would you weigh more on the planet Neptune than you do on Earth? *[Total 2]*

3 Describe how the gravitational forces acting on a spacecraft would change as it travelled from the Earth to the Moon. *[Total 3]*

4 List as many different uses of satellites as you can.

[Total 4]

5 If a geostationary satellite was accidentally knocked into a higher orbit, how would this change the time it took the satellite to orbit the Earth? *[Total 1]*

6 Figure 1 shows the Earth and the Sun (diagram not to scale).

Earth

Sun

Figure 1

a) Copy the diagram and add arrows to indicate the gravitational forces acting on the Earth and Sun. *[3]*

b) Explain why the Earth orbits the Sun. *[4]*

c) Does the Moon orbit the Sun? Explain your answer. *[3]*

[Total 10]

7 Europa is one of Jupiter's moons.
a) Why is Europa called a satellite and not a planet? *[1]*
b) What will determine the time it takes for Europa to orbit Jupiter? *[1]*

[Total 2]

8 a) Give examples of some ways life would be easier while living on the Moon. *[3]*
b) How do you think living on the Moon would affect a child's muscle development? *[3]*

[Total 6]

9 Some students say that the Sun is burning. Explain why this statement is incorrect. *[Total 3]*

10 Imagine a new dwarf planet has been discovered beyond Pluto. Give some details about it. You should be able to say what temperature it might have, how long it takes to orbit the Sun, and why you think it has taken so long to discover this body.

[Total 5]

11 Choose your answers to these questions from this list:
galaxy   planet   asteroid
moon   Sun   satellite
a) Which two objects orbit a planet? *[1]*
b) Which object is a star? *[1]*
c) Which object is the largest? *[1]*
d) Which object can be found between Mars and Jupiter? *[1]*
e) Which object describes the Earth? *[1]*

[Total 5]

12 How does the orbit of a comet differ from the orbit of a planet? *[Total 4]*

13 The Earth and the Moon are in the same region of the solar system, so you would expect that similar numbers of meteorites or asteroids would hit them. Suggest two reasons why there are many more impact craters visible on the Moon than on the Earth. *[Total 4]*

14 Communication satellites for satellite television are placed in geostationary orbits.
a) How long does it take a geostationary satellite to orbit the Earth? *[1]*
b) Why is it important for these satellites to be in geostationary orbits? *[2]*
[Total 3]

15 Mercury is the closest planet to the Sun, but its mean temperature is only 67 °C. Why is this? *[Total 2]*

16 Spending probes to other planets and sending
R astronauts to the International Space Station costs a lot of money. Some people think that this money would be better spent helping people on Earth. What do you think? Give reasons for your opinions. *[Total 6]*

17 The Moon is covered in craters formed by meteorites
R hitting its surface. One way to model the formation of craters is to drop objects into a tray of sand. Plan an investigation to show how the size of craters is affected by the mass and speed of falling objects.

18 There are lots of comets. Find out about Halley's
R Comet and Shoemaker-Levy 9.

19 a) What conditions are necessary for life forms
R to survive? *[2]*
b) What evidence would you look for in searching for life? *[2]*
c) Which two bodies in the solar system, apart from the Earth do scientists think are the most likely places for life to have formed? *[2]*
[Total 6]

20 Find out about the Mars rovers Spirit and
R Opportunity. When were they launched, what can they do and what have they found out?

21 The stars can be used for navigation. Find out how
P they are used.

22 Find out why Yuri Gagarin and Neil Armstrong are
R famous. Write notes on what you found out about them and what they achieved.

23 How could people have used the Sun and Moon to
R tell the time before clocks were invented?

24 Find out about the space probes *Galileo* and *Cassini*.
R When were they launched, where did they go and what did they find out?

25 Stars like our Sun will not last forever. What will
R happen to the Sun as its energy runs out?

26 Find out how some of the star constellations got
R their names.

4.1 Motion and speed

How can we calculate how fast an object is moving? How long will a journey take at a particular **speed**? Speed is a measure of how fast something is moving. The speed of an object tells us the distance it travels each second.

An Olympic sprinter will run about 10 metres every second. We say they are running at a speed of 10 metres per second. This can be written as 10 m/s.

Calculating speed

To calculate speed, the distance travelled is divided by the time taken to travel that distance. During the journey the speed may change, meaning that the speed calculated in this way is the **average speed**.

> average speed = distance travelled ÷ time taken

Figure 1.1 *Usain Bolt can run the 100 metres in under 10 seconds.*

Example
A horse takes 12 s to trot a distance of 96 m. Calculate the average speed of the horse during this part of its journey.

- information:
  distance travelled = 96 m
  time taken = 12 s.

- calculation:
  average speed = distance travelled ÷ time taken
  = 96 m ÷ 12 s
  = 8 m/s.

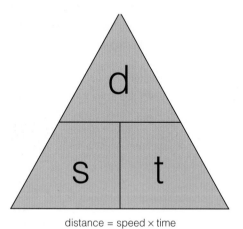

distance = speed × time

Figure 1.2 *Equation triangle.*

Distance travelled

To calculate the distance travelled you need to know the time taken for the journey and the average speed during the journey. You can then calculate the distance travelled using the following equation (see equation triangle in Figure 1.2):

> distance travelled = average speed × time taken

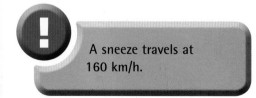

A sneeze travels at 160 km/h.

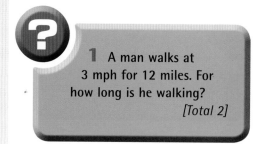

Example
A girl walks at an average speed of 2 m/s for 80 s. Calculate how far she walked in that time.

○ information:
  average speed = 2 m/s
  time taken = 80 s.

○ calculation:
  distance travelled = average speed × time taken
  = 2 m/s × 80 s
  = 160 m.

?

1 A man walks at 3 mph for 12 miles. For how long is he walking?
[Total 2]

Time taken

To calculate the time taken to travel a given distance when the average speed is known, use the following equation (see equation triangle in Figure 1.2):

time taken = distance travelled ÷ average speed

Example
A ferry transports cars across a river at an average speed of 4 m/s. The river is 640 m wide. Calculate the time that it takes for the ferry to cross the river.

○ information:
  distance travelled = 640 m
  average speed = 4 m/s.

○ calculation:
  time taken = distance travelled ÷ average speed
  = 640 m ÷ 4 s
  = 160 s.

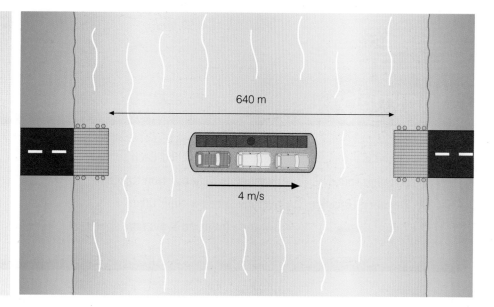

Figure 1.3 *Car ferry crossing a river.*

Other units of speed

It is not always a good idea to measure speeds in metres per second. A snail making its way along a garden path will be moving very slowly and it would be better to measure its speed in millimetres per second.

For a car travelling along a motorway at high speed it would be better to measure the speed in miles per hour (mph) or kilometres per hour (km/h).

The same equation is used to calculate the speed, but the appropriate units for distance and time must be used. To find the speed of the snail (mm/s) the distance should be measured in millimetres and the time in seconds. To find the speed of a car in kilometres per hour, the distance travelled should be measured in kilometres and the time taken measured in hours.

? 2 Write down four different units that can be used for speed. *[Total 4]*

> *Example*
> A motorbike travelled from Reading to Cardiff along the M4 motorway. The distance travelled was 186 km and the time taken for the journey was 2 h. Calculate the average speed of the motorbike.
>
> ○ information:
> distance travelled = 186 km
> time taken = 2.0 h.
> ○ calculation:
> average speed = distance travelled ÷ time taken
> = 186 km ÷ 2.0 h
> = 93 km/h.

Summary

- ○ Speed is a measure of the distance travelled each second.
- ○ Average speed   = distance travelled ÷ time taken.
- ○ Distance travelled   = average speed × time taken.
- ○ Time taken   = distance travelled ÷ average speed.

Questions

1 To calculate speed, you need to know the _____ travelled and the _____ taken. Speed can be measured in metres per _____. For cars more appropriate units are _____ per hour. *[Total 2]*

2 A man walks a distance of 2 m every second.
 a) What speed is he travelling at? *[1]*
 b) How far will he have walked in:
  i) 5 s
  ii) 50 s
  iii) 2 min
  iv) 2 hr? *[4]*
 [Total 5]

3 A sprint cyclist travels 500 m in 20 s. Calculate her average speed. *[Total 3]*

4 A tortoise takes 50 s to move 800 cm across a lawn. Calculate the tortoise's average speed. *[Total 3]*

5 A cat falls out of a tree, dropping 3.2 m in 0.8 s.
 a) Calculate the cat's average speed during the fall. *[3]*
 b) Explain why it is important to refer to this as the cat's average speed. *[2]*
 [Total 5]

6 While travelling at 30 m/s along a motorway, the driver of a car shuts his eyes for 4 s. Calculate the distance travelled by the car during this time. *[Total 3]*

7 A boat is cruising along a river at a speed of 3 m/s. Calculate the time it takes the boat to travel a distance of 270 m. *[Total 3]*

8 If a snail travelled at an average speed of 1.5 mm/s, how long would it take for the snail to:
 a) travel 30 mm *[3]*
 b) cross an 80 cm wide path? *[3]*
 [Total 6]

9 An Intercity train travels at an average speed of 160 km/h. How long will it take the train to travel:
 a) 80 km *[2]*
 b) 800 km *[2]*
 c) 100 miles? (1 mile = 1600 metres.) *[2]*
 [Total 6]

10 A Grand Prix racing car has an average lap speed of 180 km/h. Each lap is 4.5 km. How many laps will it complete in 1.5 hours? *[Total 4]*

11 A dog chased a cat across a farm field. The dog was running at a speed of 13 m/s, while the cat was travelling at 11 m/s. The cat started the chase 16 m ahead of the dog and was 77 m from the safety of an oak tree. Calculate whether or not the dog caught the cat. *[Total 6]*

4.2 Motion graphs

Can we use graphs to show how something is moving? There is more than one way of using graphs to show the motion of an object.

Farshad's journey

Farshad walked to the shops to buy some batteries for his personal stereo. His journey can be described like this:

A The shop was 600 m from his home and it took 300 s for Farshad to walk there.

B He spent 240 s in the shop buying the batteries and fitting them into his personal stereo.

C He then walked back home listening to some music. This took Farshad 400 s.

Another way to describe this journey is to use a **distance–time graph**.

- Section A is a straight line that shows Farshad is travelling at a steady speed.
- Section B is a horizontal line showing that he is not moving.
- Section C is a straight line but it is not quite as steep as section A. This shows that Farshad is travelling at a steady speed but slightly slower than during section A.

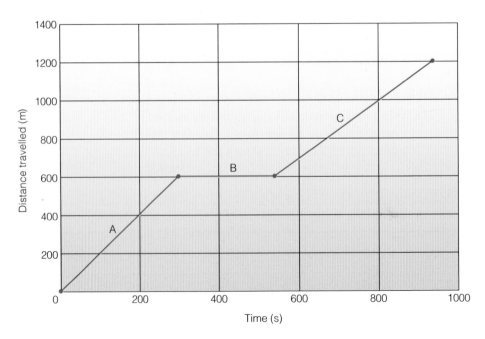

Figure 2.1 *Farshad's journey.*

The graph also gives the information that is needed to calculate Farshad's speed during each part of his journey. This is shown in Table 2.1.

Examples of distance–time graphs

Figure 2.2 shows three examples of distance–time graphs. Figure 2.2a shows an object that is stationary; Figure 2.2b shows an object that is moving at a steady speed and Figure 2.2c shows an object that is moving faster and faster, or accelerating.

Speed–time graphs

Figure 2.3 shows the speed of a tractor travelling at a steady speed of 6 m/s. When an object is travelling at a steady speed, plotting a **speed–time graph** produces a horizontal straight line.

Table 2.1 *Farshad's speed during his journey.*

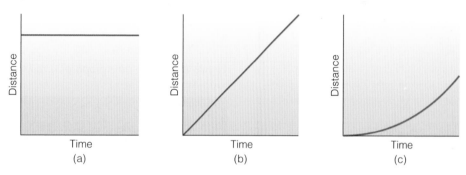

	A	B	C
Distance travelled (m)	600	0	600
Time taken (s)	300	240	400
Speed (m/s)	= 600 ÷ 300	= 0 ÷ 240	= 600 ÷ 400
	= 2	= 0	= 1.5

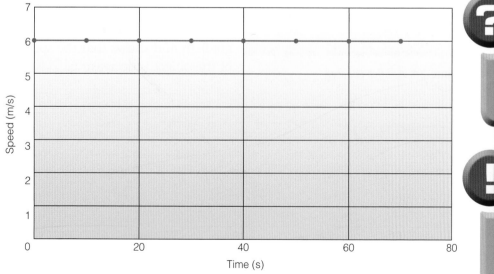

Figure 2.2 *Three distance–time graphs: a) stationary object; b) object moving at a steady speed; c) object getting faster (or accelerating).*

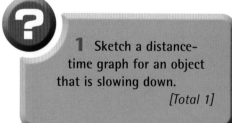

1 Sketch a distance-time graph for an object that is slowing down.
[Total 1]

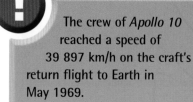

The crew of *Apollo 10* reached a speed of 39 897 km/h on the craft's return flight to Earth in May 1969.

Figure 2.3 *Speed–time graph for tractor going at a steady speed of 6 m/s.*

Table 2.2 *Speed of a roller coaster.*

Time (s)	Speed (m/s)
0	4
2	4
4	4
6	4
8	4
10	4
12	4
14	4
16	7
18	15
20	23
22	31
24	33
26	31
28	23
30	15
32	7
34	7

Table 2.2 and Figure 2.4 show the speed of a roller coaster. The first part shows it being pulled up the first slope at a steady speed. It speeds up as it rolls down the first dip and slows down again when it rises up the other side.

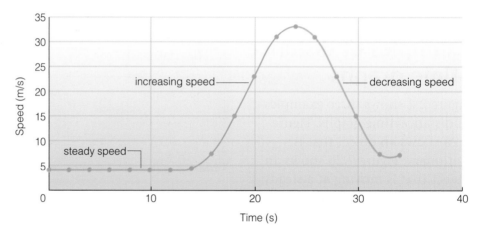

Figure 2.4 *Speed–time graph of a roller coaster.*

Figure 2.5 *A roller coaster.*

Examples of speed–time graphs

Figure 2.6 shows three examples of speed–time graphs. Figure 2.6a shows an object that is moving at a steady speed; Figure 2.6b has a positive gradient and shows an object whose speed is increasing and Figure 2.6c has a negative gradient and shows that the speed of the object is decreasing.

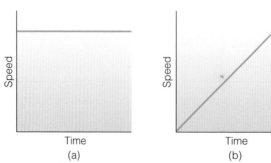

Figure 2.6 *Three speed–time graphs: a) object moving at a steady speed; b) speed of object increasing; c) speed of object decreasing.*

Summary

Distance–time graphs

- A straight horizontal line means the object is not moving.
- A straight line at an angle to the horizontal means the object is moving at a steady speed.
- A curved line means the object is speeding up or slowing down.

Speed–time graphs

- A straight horizontal line means the object is moving at a steady speed.
- A straight line with a positive gradient means the object is speeding up.
- A straight line with a negative gradient means the object is slowing down.

Questions

1 Distance-_____ graphs can be used to describe a journey. If something is not moving the line will be a straight _____ line. If something is moving at a steady _____, the graph will be a straight _____. *[Total 2]*

2 Look at Figure 2.7. Which graphs are for objects that are:
a) not moving *[1]*
b) moving at a steady speed *[2]*
c) slowing down *[2]*
d) speeding up? *[1]*
[Total 6]

3 Figure 2.8 shows Ceri's walk to school.
a) How far does Ceri live from the school? *[2]*
b) How long did she stop for? *[2]*
c) What was Ceri's speed for each part of the journey? *[3]*
d) Write a story about Ceri's walk to school so that the story fits with the distance–time graph for her journey. *[6]*
[Total 13]

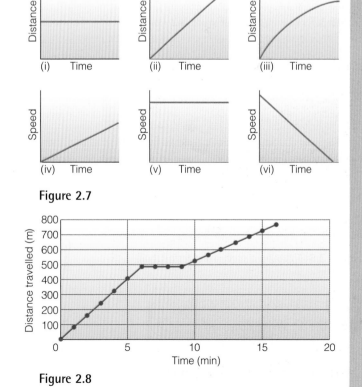

Figure 2.7

Figure 2.8

4.3 Forces

How can we measure a force? What happens when more than one force is applied to an object? We make use of forces all around us to carry out everyday activities. Many things are subject to more than one force.

Everyday forces

Most forces that we use either push or pull on something. A force can also be used to change the shape of an object. When a force is applied to a moving object it may cause the object to speed up, slow down or change direction. Figures 3.1–3.5 show forces in use around us.

Figure 3.1 *Pushing a bowling ball.*   **Figure 3.2** *Pulling a water skier.*   **Figure 3.3** *Squashing a balloon.*   **Figure 3.4** *Twisting a bottle top.*   **Figure 3.5** *Supporting a child.*

Figure 3.6 *Applying a force to a tennis ball.*

A tennis player applies a force to the ball using a racket. The ball will be squashed as it is hit and it will also change direction. The ball may also speed up or be forced to spin.

Measuring forces

One device that can be used to measure forces is a **newton meter**. A newton meter can be used to weigh an object. It can also be used to measure other pulling forces such as the force needed to pull open a drawer. The unit of force is the **newton** (N) and was named after Sir Isaac Newton.

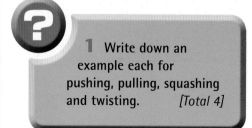

1 Write down an example each for pushing, pulling, squashing and twisting. *[Total 4]*

Weight

If someone were to stand on your stomach you would feel a force pushing down on you. This downward force is called **weight**. Weight is a force, so like other forces it is measured in newtons.

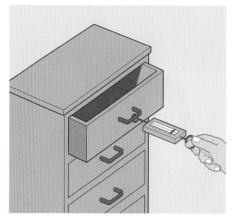

Figure 3.7 *Measuring the force needed to open a drawer with a newton meter.*

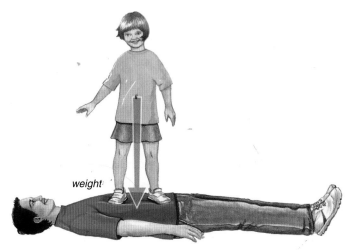

weight

Figure 3.8

Mass and weight

Mass and weight are often confused; even scientists sometimes mix them up in everyday conversations. **Mass** is a measure of the amount of matter in an object and is measured in kilograms. Weight is the downward force acting on a mass and is caused by gravity. It is measured in newtons (N).

Outside a gravitational field an object would still have mass but it would not have weight. The gravitational field on the Moon is less than the gravitational field on the Earth. This is why an object will weigh less on the Moon even though its mass has not changed.

The Earth's gravitational field strength is 10 N/kg. This means that the Earth's gravitational field pulls with a force of 10 N on each kilogram of mass.

A 1 kg mass will weigh 10 N and a man who has a mass of 80 kg will weigh 800 N on Earth.

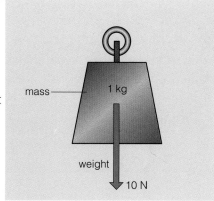

mass — 1 kg

weight

10 N

Figure 3.9

> **!** In 1990, Walter Arfeuille from Belgium lifted weights totalling 2762 N off the ground using his teeth. That is about the same weight as 28 large buckets of water.

> **?** **2** What is the weight of a 20 kg child?
>
> [Total 1]

> **!** Jon Minnoch from the USA had a body mass of 635 kg. When he was rushed to hospital after respiratory and heart failure it took 12 firemen to move him on an improvised stretcher.

Figure 3.10

?

3 Write down one place in a playground where friction is
a) useful [1]
b) not useful. [1]
[Total 2]

Friction

Friction is a force that stops things moving or causes them to move more slowly. It occurs when two surfaces are in contact with each other. Rougher surfaces produce a lot of friction and smooth surfaces produce less friction.

Friction is often very useful. Without the friction between the soles of your shoes and the ground you would find it very difficult to walk. Imagine trying to run a 100 m race on slippery ice! Friction is also useful in the brakes of a car where frictional force is used to slow the car down.

There are situations where friction is not wanted and **lubricants** are often applied to reduce the friction between two surfaces. Oil is used inside a car engine to help the moving parts move more freely and also to stop them from wearing away. Friction often causes unwanted heat energy.

Skis have flat smooth surfaces so that they slide easily over the snow. Skiers also wax their skis to reduce the friction even more.

Friction and cycling

Friction is needed on a bike to enable you to ride it, as shown in Figure 3.11. When you want to stop a bike you apply the brakes.

The brake blocks rub against the wheel to produce a frictional force that slows the wheels down. Then friction between the tyres and the road slows the bike down. Some people apply the back brake so hard that the wheel locks and the tyre skids, sometimes leaving a black skid mark caused by the tyre being worn away.

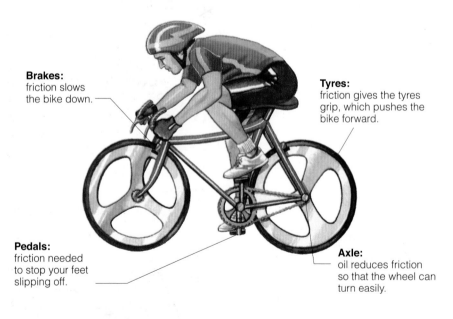

Brakes:
friction slows the bike down.

Tyres:
friction gives the tyres grip, which pushes the bike forward.

Pedals:
friction needed to stop your feet slipping off.

Axle:
oil reduces friction so that the wheel can turn easily.

Figure 3.11 *How friction is used on a bicycle.*

! When investigating road accidents, the police measure the length of skid marks to help them decide how fast each car was moving.

Drag

When an object is moving through a gas or liquid it experiences an opposing force called **drag**. Drag is caused by friction between the liquid or gas and the surface of the object that is moving through it. You may have experienced this when you have put your hand out of the window of a moving car. As an object moves faster through a liquid or gas, the drag acting on it increases.

Air resistance

The drag caused when an object moves through air is called **air resistance**. Cars, rockets and cycling helmets all have streamlined shapes to reduce air resistance.

It is very important for the back of the car to also have a streamlined shape. If the air does not pass smoothly over the back of the car it creates an area of low pressure

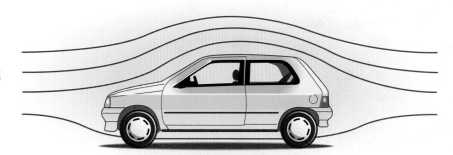

Figure 3.12 *Streamlined shapes move smoothly through the air.*

behind the car, slowing the car down. High velocity bullets also have a tapered back to help them travel faster through the air.

A streamlined shape means the car can travel faster but more importantly it means the car is more efficient and will use less fuel during a journey.

Cars that break world speed records are very streamlined but when it is time to stop they dramatically increase the air resistance by releasing a parachute behind them.

Figure 3.13 Thrust SSC *using its parachutes to stop.*

When spacecraft re-enter the Earth's atmosphere they are in danger of burning up due to friction from the air. The Space Shuttle has a thermal protection system made of various materials applied to its outer surfaces.

4 Why are streamlined cars better for the environment? [Total 2]

More than one force

Opposing forces

If two equal forces are applied to a stationary object in opposite directions, the object does not move. The two forces balance each other out and are called **balanced forces**.

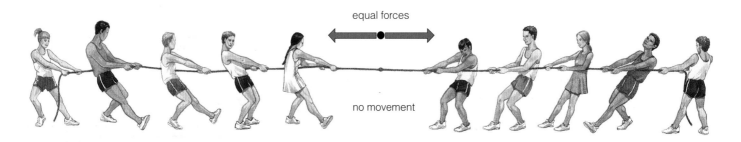

Figure 3.14 *Balanced forces.*

A tug of war contest involves two teams attempting to pull the other team 4 m towards them.

If one force is greater than the other, the object will move in the direction of the larger force.

We can calculate the effect of opposing forces if we know the size of the forces. If the forces are acting in opposite directions, one can be subtracted from the other to give a resultant, or net, force.

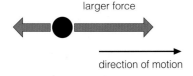

Figure 3.15 *Unbalanced forces.*

> *Example*
> The block shown in Figure 3.16 has two opposing forces being applied to it: 7 N to the right and 4 N to the left. To calculate the effect, subtract one from the other:
> 7 N – 4 N = 3 N to the right.

Figure 3.16

Forces in balance

When a man stands on a table, if he does not move downwards there must be an upward force from the table to balance the downward force of his weight.

Example

A man of mass of 75 kg has a weight of 750 N. This 750 N weight will act downwards on the table and the table will exert a 750 N force upwards on the man. The table bends a little until it can exert the required upward force, stretching like the string on a bow and arrow.

If the upward force were less than 750 N, the man would move downwards.

Any object that is not moving must have balanced forces acting upon it.

Figure 3.17

Sinking and floating

When a boat is floating on the water there is a force called **upthrust** keeping it afloat. The volume of water displaced by the boat creates the upthrust. The more water displaced, the greater the upthrust.

Adding weight to a boat will cause it to sink down into the water until the upthrust is equal to the total weight of the boat again. When the total weight is greater than the maximum upthrust the boat can create, the boat sinks.

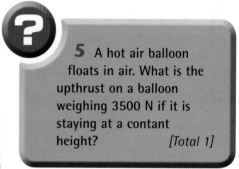

5 A hot air balloon floats in air. What is the upthrust on a balloon weighing 3500 N if it is staying at a contant height? [Total 1]

Figure 3.18 The balanced forces acting upon a boat

Free fall

The moment you jump off a table there is only one force acting upon you: your weight. You will then **accelerate** downwards until there is an upward force exerted upon your body by the floor. Jumping from a table to the floor would take less than one second and you would only reach a speed of a few metres per second. The air resistance at such a low speed would be very small.

Jumping from an aeroplane is a different story. As you fall your speed increases and the air resistance acting on your body gets greater and greater. Eventually you will reach a speed where the air resistance is equal to your weight. The upward and downward forces are then balanced and you carry on going down at a steady speed called the **terminal velocity**.

Increasing the air resistance by opening a parachute greatly reduces your terminal velocity, enabling you to land safely.

Figure 3.19 Balanced forces on a parachute.

When a DC-9 airliner blew up over Czechoslovakia in 1972, Yugoslavian air stewardess Vesna Vulovic survived a fall of over 10 km without a parachute.

Approximate terminal velocities when you are in free fall are:
- falling head first: 290 km/h
- falling horizontally: 190 km/h
- with a parachute open: 8 km/h.

When the forces are balanced you will not speed up and you will not slow down; this is why you carry on moving downward at a steady speed.

Balanced forces on moving objects

A car moving at a constant speed has forces of air resistance and friction acting to slow it down. It needs a forward force from its engine to balance these forces. If the forwards and backwards forces are balanced, the car will continue to move at a constant speed.

If the forces on a moving object are balanced, it will continue to move in a straight line at a constant speed.

6 Why does an aeroplane need to use its engines when it is flying level at a steady speed?

[Total 1]

Summary

- Forces are used to push, pull, turn, squash, stretch and support objects.
- Forces make objects move, slow down, speed up and change direction.
- The newton is a unit of force.
- Forces can be measured using a newton meter.
- Weight is the downward force acting on a mass in a gravitational field.
- Friction occurs when two surfaces are in contact with each other and can be reduced using lubricants such as oil.
- Friction is useful for grip and for braking moving objects. Friction reduces the speed of moving objects, creates unwanted heat energy and causes moving parts to wear out.
- Using streamlined shapes can reduce air resistance.
- An object that is not moving has balanced forces applied to it.
- A moving object with balanced forces acting on it will travel in a straight line at a steady speed.

Questions

1 Forces can be measured using a _____ meter and are measured in _____. If an object is not moving, forces are _____. If an object is moving at a steady _____, the forces are balanced. *[Total 2]*

2 a) Explain the meaning of the words mass and weight. Take care to highlight the differences between the two. *[4]*

b) Table 3.1 shows the relationship between mass and weight on Earth. Copy and complete the table. *[4]*

[Total 8]

Table 3.1

Mass (kg)	Weight (N)
1	10
2	
10	
15	150
	500
200	

3 Give three examples of where:

a) friction is useful *[3]*

b) friction is not useful. *[3]*

[Total 6]

4 After about 20 000 km of use, engine oil is no longer as good as new engine oil at lubricating a car engine. Explain why a car engine might develop problems if the oil is not changed when the car is serviced. *[Total 3]*

5 a) What is the difference between the two lorries shown in Figure 3.20? *[1]*

b) What advantages does lorry B have over lorry A? *[3]*

[Total 4]

Figure 3.20

6 Look at the forces applied to each object in Figure 3.21.

i) 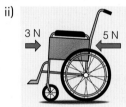 ii)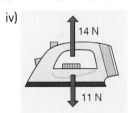

iii) 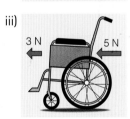 iv)

v)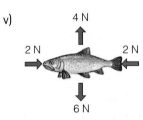

Figure 3.21

a) What is the resultant force acting on each object? *[5]*

b) In which direction will each object move? *[5]*

[Total 10]

4.4 More about forces

Why does using a lever make it easier to lift a heavy object? Why do your ears sometimes hurt when you swim under water? Forces can be used to turn things, and they can act on us from all directions. **Pressure** is a form of force that is applied over a certain area.

Stretching springs

The English physicist Robert Hooke made many significant contributions to the development of physics, but he is most famous for the relatively simple relationship called **Hooke's law**.

We can see Hooke's law in action when masses are hung on the end of a spring, as in Figure 4.1. Each 100 g of mass hung on the spring will apply a force of 1.0 N that stretches the spring. Each time an extra 1.0 N force is applied, the length of the spring will increase by the same amount.

The length of the spring without any force applied to it is called the **original length**. The total increase in length of the spring is called the **extension**.

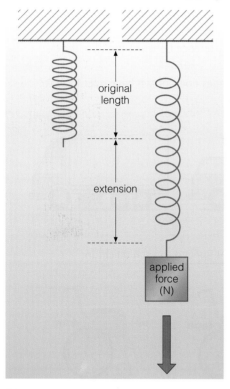

Figure 4.1

> extension = new length − original length

> Hooke's law states that the extension of a spring is directly proportional to the force applied to it.

Plotting a graph of extension against the force applied produces a straight line until the spring is stretched beyond its **elastic limit**, as shown in Figure 4.2.

The elastic limit is the point at which the force applied is too great for the spring and it no longer returns to its original length when the force is removed. If the spring is stretched beyond the elastic limit, it no longer obeys Hooke's law.

?

1 A spring has a weight of 5 N hanging on it, and an extension of 10 cm. What will the extension be if the weight is 10 N ?   *[Total 1]*

!

Springs are big business. Manufacturers earn millions of pounds by making springs of all different shapes and sizes. Springs are used in many different machines from watches to train suspension systems.

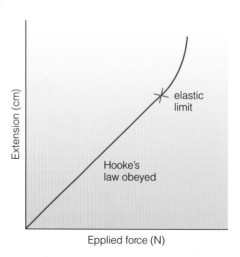

Figure 4.2 *Hooke's law graph for a spring.*

Metal wires also obey Hooke's law until they reach their elastic limits.

Turning forces

Door handles, spanners and bicycle pedals all use a lever effect to turn an object. Using a longer lever means that less force is needed to produce the same turning effect. To undo a nut, a given turning effect is needed to make it turn. This can be achieved more easily using a smaller force at a greater distance.

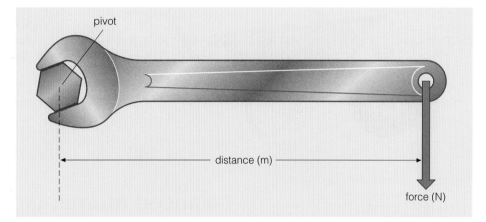

Figure 4.3 *The moment produced by using a spanner to tighten a nut.*

The turning effect of a force is called a **moment**. The moment is calculated by multiplying the force by the distance from the **pivot** (see the equation triangle shown in Figure 4.4).

> moment (N m) = force (N) × distance (m)

The force is sometimes called the **effort**. Using a long spanner increases the moment applied by the force, as the distance is longer and creates a greater turning effect at the pivot point.

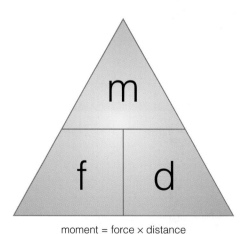

moment = force × distance

Figure 4.4 *Equation triangle for moment, force and distance.*

This principle of moments is used in many everyday situations, such as turning on a tap, opening a bottle of drink, using a lever to open a tin of paint or transporting heavy objects in a wheelbarrow. Using a lever to open a tin of paint applies a larger force to the lid than you do to the lever.

Sometimes the force is not acting straight down or straight up. To calculate the moment correctly, the force should be acting in a direction that is perpendicular to the distance. This means that the force needs to be at a right angle to a line drawn from the pivot point to where the force is applied.

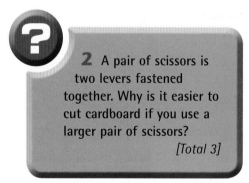

2 A pair of scissors is two levers fastened together. Why is it easier to cut cardboard if you use a larger pair of scissors?

[Total 3]

Figure 4.5 *Moment produced by using a wheelbarrow.*

Example
Look at the wheelbarrow shown in Figure 4.5. The moment can be calculated as follows:

● information
force = 200 N
distance = 1.8 m.

● calculation
moment = force × distance
= 200 N × 1.8 m
= 360 N m.

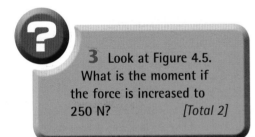

3 Look at Figure 4.5. What is the moment if the force is increased to 250 N? *[Total 2]*

Balanced moments

Two people of different weights can successfully balance a seesaw if the lighter person sits further from the pivot than the heavier person. By sitting at a greater distance they make their moment equal to the moment of the heavier person.

Example
Look at the seesaw in shown in Figure 4.6. The moments can be calculated as follows:

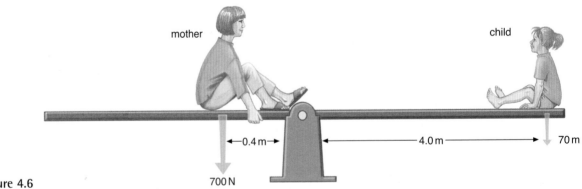

Figure 4.6

Mother
● information
force = 700 N
distance = 0.4 m.
● calculation
moment = force × distance
= 700 N × 0.4 m
= 280 N m.

Child
● information
force = 70 N
distance = 4.0 m.
● calculation
moment = force × distance
= 70 N × 4.0 m
= 280 N m.

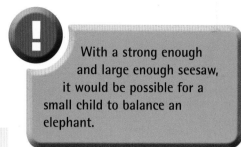

The seesaw is balanced because the two moments are equal in size and they are trying to turn the seesaw in opposite directions. The weight of the mother would turn the seesaw in an anticlockwise direction and is called the **anticlockwise moment**. The weight of the child would turn the seesaw the other way and is called a **clockwise moment**.

> **!** With a strong enough and large enough seesaw, it would be possible for a small child to balance an elephant.

> When balanced, anticlockwise moment = clockwise moment

With a pivot point at one end rather than in the middle, the principle of moments still applies.

Look at Figure 4.7. The strongman is much further from the pivot than the woman. This makes it easier for him to support her weight than might be imagined.

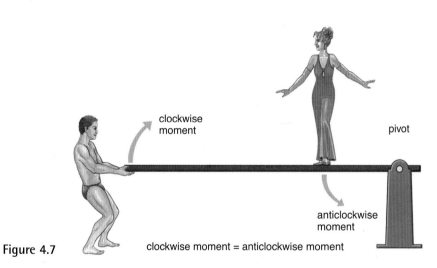

Figure 4.7

clockwise moment = anticlockwise moment

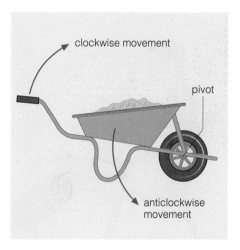

Figure 4.8

A wheelbarrow works on the same principle, as shown in Figure 4.8.

Pressure

Pressure is a way of saying how concentrated a force is. The pressure exerted on an object depends upon the force applied to it and the area the force is applied to.

Pressure and area

Sitting on a chair is more comfortable than sitting on a fence because your weight is applied to a larger area, as shown in Figure 4.9. The flesh on your bottom also helps to spread your weight out when you sit down.

> **?** 4 The woman in Figure 4.7 weighs 600 N and is standing 1 m from the pivot. The man is 3.5 m from the pivot. What force is he exerting? [Total 4]

Figure 4.10 *Less downward force – less pressure.*

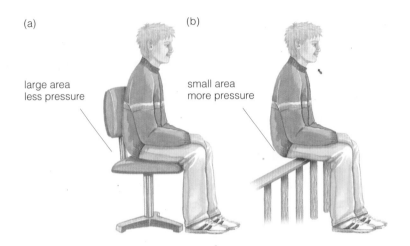

(a) large area less pressure

(b) small area more pressure

Figure 4.9 *a) The cushion on a chair spreads your weight out over a larger **area**. This feels more comfortable because there is less **pressure**. b) Sitting on a fence concentrates your weight onto a smaller **area**. The fence is uncomfortable because there is more **pressure**.*

Pressure and force

Increasing the force will increase the pressure. A chair placed on snow would sink a small distance into the snow. If you then sat on the chair, this would increase the downward force and increase the pressure, causing the chair to sink deeper into the snow, as shown in Figures 4.10 and 4.11.

Calculating pressure

To calculate pressure, the force exerted is divided by the area that the force is exerted over (see equation triangle in Figure 4.12).

pressure = force ÷ area

Figure 4.11 *More downward force – more pressure.*

The pascal is a unit of pressure named after the seventeenth century French physicist, Blaise Pascal.
1 pascal = 1 N/m².

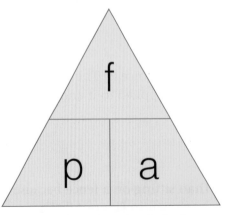

Figure 4.12 *Equation triangle for force, pressure and area.*

Example 1

A dancer stands on tiptoe with only one foot touching the floor. She weighs
500 N. The area of contact between her foot and the floor is 10 cm^2.
What pressure does she exert on the floor?

○ information
  force = 500 N.
  area = 10 cm^2.

○ calculation
  pressure = force ÷ area
  = 500 N ÷ 10 cm^2
  = 50 N/cm^2.

Note: the area was measured in cm^2. So the unit of pressure used
is N/cm^2.

Example 2

Calculate the pressure exerted on the floor by a filing cabinet weighing 420 N.
The dimensions of the filing cabinet are shown in Figure 4.14.

○ information
  height = 1.2 m
  width = 0.5 m
  depth = 0.6 m
  force = 420 N.

○ calculations
  area in contact with the floor
  = width × depth
  = 0.5 m × 0.6 m
  = 0.3 m^2.
  pressure = force ÷ area
  = 420 N ÷ 0.3 m^2
  = 1400 N/m^2.

Note: the area was measured in m^2. So the unit of pressure used is N/m^2.

Figure 4.13

The dancer standing on tiptoe exerts a pressure of 50 N/cm^2. This is
equal to a pressure of 500 000 N/m^2, more than 350 times greater than
the pressure exerted by the filing cabinet.

Pressure in liquids and gases

Pressure in liquids

When swimming under water, you may have felt the pressure from
the water above you making your eardrums hurt. The pressure in
liquids increases with depth. This means that dams need to be
thicker at the bottom than they are at the top (Figure 4.15). If they
were not, the bottom of the dam might collapse because of the much
higher pressure there.

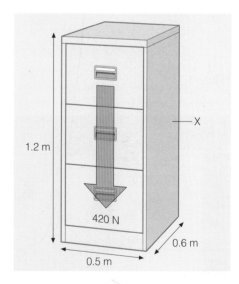

Figure 4.14

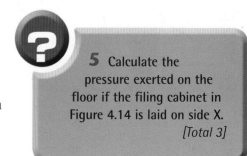

?

5 Calculate the
pressure exerted on the
floor if the filing cabinet in
Figure 4.14 is laid on side X.
[Total 3]

The increase in pressure caused by greater depth of water can easily be shown using a can with holes drilled in the sides.

The pressure is greater at the bottom of the can due to the weight of water pushing down from above. This produces a faster jet of water at the bottom. The jet of water at the bottom travels further than the jet of water at the top, as shown in Figure 4.16.

Pressure acts in all directions

The pressure does not only push downward: water pressure and air pressure act in all directions. If you were face down in the middle of a pile of people, you would feel as much pressure on your front as you would on your back. This also means that you could not escape from high pressures under water by swimming into a cave. The pressure depends on the depth of water you are in. The rock above you would not shield you from this pressure.

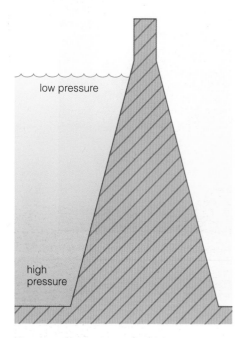

Figure 4.15

Figure 4.16

Figure 4.17 *The pressure acting on the fish is the same as the pressure acting on the scuba diver.*

Pressure in gases

A balloon stays inflated because the air on the inside is at a higher pressure than the air on the outside. The pressure inside the balloon balances the combined forces from the elasticity of the balloon and the air pressure outside the balloon. The pressure inside the balloon is caused by thousands of air molecules continuously hitting the wall of the balloon. More particles are hitting each square centimentre of the inside of the balloon then are hitting the same area on the outside.

The molecules in a gas are a long way apart, making it easy to compress the air by squashing the balloon with your hands.

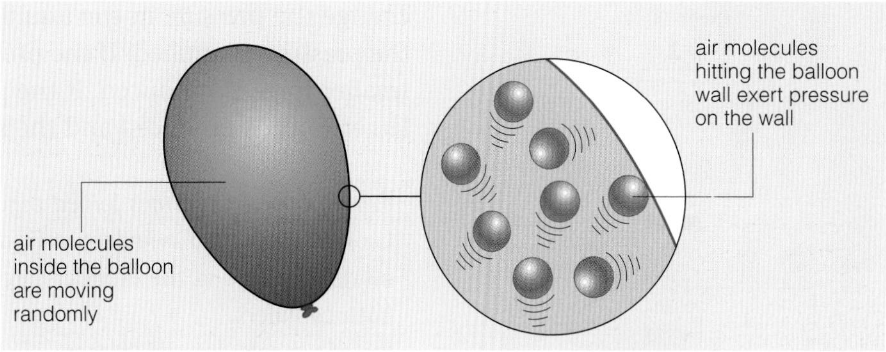

Atmospheric pressure

The air pressure at sea level is about 100 000 N/m^2. This is called **atmospheric pressure**. Atmospheric pressure at different places around the world varies a lot and is very dependent on weather conditions.

Figure 4.18 *Air pressure in a balloon.*

air molecules inside the balloon are moving randomly

air molecules hitting the balloon wall exert pressure on the wall

The Earth's atmosphere gradually gets less **dense** the higher you go. As you go higher the air pressure gets less and less. There is not a clear boundary between the Earth's atmosphere and space: the Earth's atmosphere gradually fades away into nothing.

To climb high mountains such as Mount Everest, most climbers take oxygen cylinders with them to help them breathe. The cabins of aeroplanes are pressurised so that when they fly at high altitude the air pressure is not too low. They are pressurised at the same pressure as you would be at the top of a 3000 m mountain.

> **!** At an altitude of 10 km the atmospheric pressure is reduced to about 26% of its value at sea level. The summit of Mount Everest is almost 9 km above sea level. This is why many climbing expeditions carry oxygen tanks to get to the top of Mount Everest.

Hydraulic systems

The braking system on a bike uses a lever system. The force applied to the brake lever is converted by the lever system into a larger force that slows down the moving wheel by friction. A braking system like this is called a **force multiplier**.

To slow down a car, the brakes need to apply very large forces. During the early stages of car development, lever systems were used for the brakes. As cars got faster and faster lever systems were replaced by **hydraulic systems**.

How hydraulic systems work

Liquids are very difficult to compress because the molecules are very close together. The pressure applied at one end of a liquid sealed inside a cylinder is transferred all the way along to the other end.

Linking cylinders of different diameters together enables the force to be increased or decreased. Changing the diameter of the cylinder does not

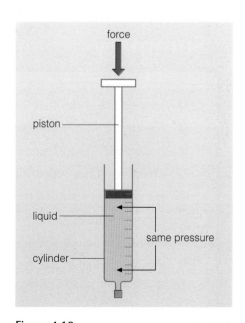

Figure 4.19

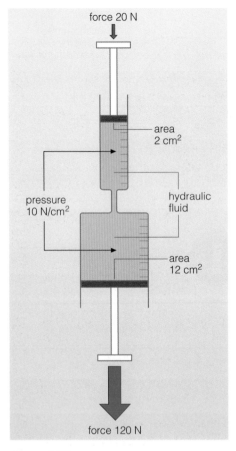

force 20 N

area
2 cm²

pressure
10 N/cm²

hydraulic
fluid

area
12 cm²

force 120 N

Figure 4.20

change the pressure in the liquid but it does change the area to which the pressure is applied. If the pressure is applied to a smaller area, a smaller force is produced. If the pressure is applied to a larger area, a larger force is produced and the system acts as a force multiplier.

Example – two syringes joined together
Look at the joined cylinders in Figure 4.20. As pressure acts equally in all directions, and the cylinders are linked, the pressure is the same in both cylinders.
But if we calculate the forces:

- force in top cylinder
  pressure = force ÷ area
  = 20 N ÷ 2 cm²
  = 10 N/cm².

- force in bottom cylinder
  force = pressure × area
  = 10 N/cm² × 12 cm²
  = 120 N.

The area of the second cylinder is six times larger than the area of the first and the hydraulic system multiplies the force by a factor of six. However, although the force is smaller, the first piston will need to be pushed six times further than the distance the second piston moves.

Hydraulic systems are also used as a force multiplier in powerful cutting tools and to lift heavy weights. If bubbles of air get into the hydraulic fluid the system does not work efficiently because the air bubbles are compressible and get squashed rather than transmitting all of the pressure. This is because the molecules in gases are further apart and so gases are easier to compress.

Summary

- Hooke's law states that the extension of a spring is directly proportional to the force applied to it.
- The elastic limit is the point beyond which Hooke's law is no longer obeyed.
- A moment is the turning effect of a force.
- Moment = force × perpendicular distance.
- For a balanced seesaw, the clockwise moment equals the anticlockwise moment.
- Pressure = force ÷ area.
- Pressure in liquids and gases increases as the depth increases.
- Pressure in liquids and gases acts in all directions.
- Hydraulic systems use liquids to transfer pressure and multiply the force.

Questions

1 Copy and complete the following sentences.
Hooke's law states that when a spring is stretched the _____ is directly _____ to the force applied to it. When stretched beyond its _____ limit the spring will no longer obey _____ law. *[Total 2]*

2 Some students performed a stretching experiment on a long spring. They obtained the results shown in Table 4.1.

Table 4.1

Force (N)	1.0	2.0	3.0	4.0	5.0	6.0	7.0	8.0	9.0	10.0
Extension (cm)	1.2	2.4	3.6	5.8	6.0	7.2	8.4	10.0	12.1	16.0

a) Plot a line graph of their results. *[3]*
b) Draw a cross to show where the elastic limit was reached and label it. *[1]*
c) The students made a mistake with one of their results. Which result do you think it was? Circle this result on the graph. *[1]*
d) How much force is needed to extend the spring by 1.0 cm? *[2]*
[Total 7]

3 Jasmin held a 2 N weight on the end of rod that was 0.7 m long. Calculate the moment acting on her hand. *[Total 2]*

4 Douglas used a metre ruler and some weights to weigh a bag of money. Figure 4.21 shows the weight and distances when the ruler was balanced. Calculate the weight of the bag of money. *[Total 3]*

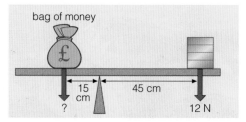
bag of money
15 cm   45 cm
?   12 N

Figure 4.21

5 Tariq measured his weight and the area of his feet: weight = 580 N; area of each foot = 130 cm².
a) Calculate the pressure Tariq exerts on the floor when he:
   i) stands on only one foot
   ii) stands with both feet on the floor. *[4]*
b) Describe one method Tariq may have used to measure the area of his feet. *[2]*
[Total 6]

6 An emergency aid parcel had been dropped by parachute into a muddy field. The parcel weighed 900 N and its dimensions were 1.5 m × 2.0 m × 3.0 m.
a) What is the greatest pressure it would exert on the ground? *[3]*
b) What is the least pressure it would exert on the ground? *[3]*
[Total 6]

7 Figure 4.22 shows a hydraulic lifting device. Calculate the lifting force produced by the device when a 40 N downward force is applied.
[Total 4]

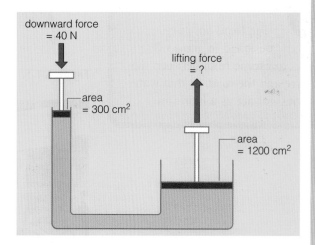
downward force = 40 N
lifting force = ?
area = 300 cm²
area = 1200 cm²

Figure 4.22

4 Forces and motion

Road safety

Engineers who design cars need to know about forces to help them to make cars safe. Drivers also need to understand why keeping to speed limits is important.

Stopping distances

When drivers see a hazard ahead, it takes them a little time to realise that they need to stop. The distance the car travels in this time is called the **thinking distance**. The faster the car is travelling, the further it goes during the thinking time.

Once the driver has pressed the brake pedal, the car starts to slow down. The distance the car travels before coming to a stop is called the **braking distance**. The overall distance travelled is the **stopping distance**. The distances shown in Figure 5.1 are based on a correctly maintained family car with good tyres, on a dry road.

?

1 The Highway Code recommends that cars travel at a distance at least as long as the stopping distance from the vehicle in front. Why is this?

[Total 1]

!

The tread on a tyre is designed to allow water to escape from between the tyre and the road, so that water does not act as a lubricant.

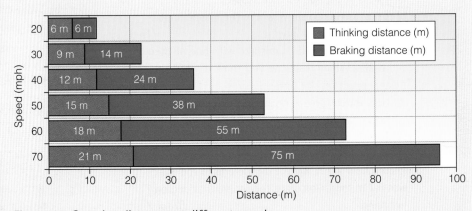

Figure 5.1 *Stopping distances at different speeds.*

Figure 5.2 *Motorway pile-ups can happen when vehicles are travelling too close together at high speed.*

Safer cars

Cars have many different features designed to reduce the number of injuries caused to the occupants if the car crashes. Most of these features are designed to reduce the deceleration of the occupants.

A change in speed is an acceleration or a deceleration. If a car comes to a very sudden stop there is a big deceleration, and the forces on the car and on the occupants are very large. If the people inside can be made to decelerate more slowly, there will be smaller forces on them and they will be less likely to be injured.

Cars are designed with 'crumple zones' at the front. These are designed to collapse if the car hits something, so the car takes longer to stop. Seatbelts also increase the time it takes the passengers to stop inside the car, so they are less likely to be injured.

Figure 5.3 *The bonnet of this car is designed to crumple when it hits something. Three of the dummies inside are not wearing seatbelts.*

2 Which dummy in the car is likely to suffer the fewest 'injuries'. Why is this? *[Total 3]*

Questions

1 Explain how the thinking and braking distances will change if
a) the driver is tired *[3]*
b) it is raining hard. *[4]*
[Total 7]

2 Explain why the speed limit is 20 mph on some housing estates, but 70 mph on motorways.
[Total 4]

3 a) Why should drivers drive slower than the maximum speed in poor visibility? *[2]*
b) Why is it important to make sure that tyres have a good tread on them? *[2]*
[Total 4]

4 a) Draw a line graph of thinking distance against speed. *[2]*
b) Is the thinking distance proportional to speed? (i.e. is the graph a straight line?) *[1]*
c) Draw a line graph of braking distance against speed. *[2]*
d) Describe how the stopping distance changes with speed. *[3]*
[Total 8]

5 Write a short article for a magazine explaining why it is a legal requirement for people to wear seatbelts in cars. Look at Figure 5.3 to help you.
[Total 4]

6 Suggest why manufacturers are required to carry out tests similar to the one in Figure 5.3 for each of their car models. *[Total 1]*

4 Forces and motion

Figure 5.4

Investigating forces and motion

Watching and measuring

People have wondered about why things move in particular ways since ancient times. Aristotle (384–322 BCE) and other Greek philosophers said that a stone thrown into the air would fall to the ground because the Earth is its natural place to be. Smoke from a fire rises because the air is above the Earth.

Aristotle also had ideas about moving objects. He said that moving things kept moving as long as there was a force on them. This idea worked well for things like carts pulled by horses, but was a bit more difficult for things that were thrown, such as arrows. In this case, the Greeks had ideas such as the air from in front of the arrow moving round behind it to keep it going. The Greeks did not do experiments to test their ideas.

It was not until the sixteenth century that scientists did experiments to find out more. We do not know if Galileo (1564–1642) really did drop objects from the leaning tower of Pisa but he certainly designed experiments to work out how things moved. He rolled balls down slopes and measured the times and distances, using a water clock. He realised that there was a force (friction) that acts to slow down moving objects. He worked out the equations for speed and acceleration that we still use today. He also worked out that if you dropped different objects, they would all fall at the same speed if there was no air resistance.

Laws of force and motion

Isaac Newton was born in Woolsthorpe, Lincolnshire on Christmas Day 1642. A well-known story suggests that Newton was sitting in his orchard when an apple fell on his head and this made him think about gravity. Whether it actually happened or not, he realised that the same force governed the motion of the Moon and the motion of a falling apple. Newton developed three fundamental laws about forces that explained Galileo's equations of motion. He also worked out how gravity could explain the way planets orbited around the sun. The unit of force was named the newton. Newton didn't tell anyone about his ideas for a number of years until he published all his work on forces in a book called *Principia*. Meanwhile, other people were thinking about forces, including Robert Hooke.

Robert Hooke was born on the Isle of Wight, England in July 1635. He is most famous for his law of elasticity, which is now known as Hooke's law. Hooke's law is vital in engineering. It allows engineers to understand stress and strain in materials. He was the first person to use balanced springs for watches, and also made improvements to pendulum clocks. In 1678 he worked out a law to describe the motion of the planets but did not fully develop his ideas mathematically. When Isaac Newton used a similar idea in *Principia*, Hooke felt that he was not given sufficient credit and this led to a bitter dispute between the two men.

Newton also had a long argument with the German mathematician Gottfried Leibniz. They had both developed a new system of mathematics called calculus which Newton used to work out his laws of motion. They both claimed to have been the first and that the other had stolen their work. In fact they had come up with the ideas independently. Newton outlived all his enemies and did his best to take all the credit for himself.

After Newton

Newton's laws are still used by engineers designing buildings, bridges, cars and rockets, but in the twentieth century Albert Einstein (1879–1955) showed that Newton hadn't worked out everything. Einstein showed that when objects are travelling extremely fast (close to the speed of light) some interesting things happen. For example Newton assumed that the mass of an object remains constant, but Einstein's theory of relativity shows that mass increases as an object accelerates to extremely large speeds.

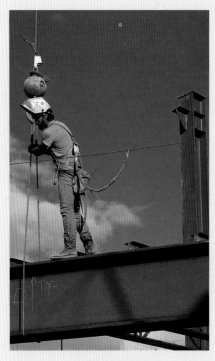

Figure 5.5 *Engineers need to understand stress and strain so they can design girders that do not bend.*

Questions

1 What is the difference between the way that Aristotle and Galileo came up with their scientific ideas?   *[Total 2]*

2 What is Galileo's equation which links speed, time and distance?   *[Total 1]*

3 Explain what Hooke's law is. Draw a graph to help you explain it.   *[Total 2]*

4 Galileo's experiments showed that Aristotle's theories of motion were wrong. Why is experimenting necessary in science?   *[Total 2]*

5
R Find out how the astronaut Dave Scott showed that Galileo's idea about objects falling without air resistance was correct.   *[Total 2]*

Applications of forces

Flying forces

There are four main forces that act upon an aeroplane, as shown in Figure 5.6:

- the weight of the aeroplane
- the **lift** from the wings as it moves through the air
- the forward **thrust** from the engines
- the drag from the air it is passing through.

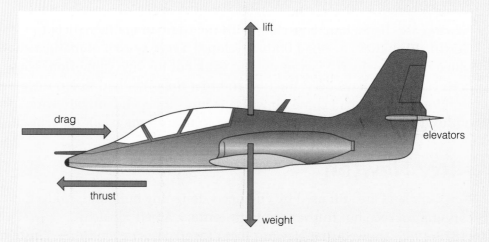

Figure 5.6

When an aeroplane is flying horizontally:

- if the aeroplane is not moving upwards and it is not moving downwards, lift = weight
- if the aeroplane is not speeding up and it is not slowing down, thrust = drag.

To speed up the pilot must increase the thrust from the engines. As the aeroplane accelerates the drag will increase until the aeroplane reaches a speed where the drag is equal to the new thrust and the aeroplane stops accelerating.

To make the aeroplane move upwards the pilot must increase the lift. Changing the shape of the wing, increasing the surface area of the wing or going faster can all increase the lift. While the lift is greater than the weight, the aeroplane will continue to rise.

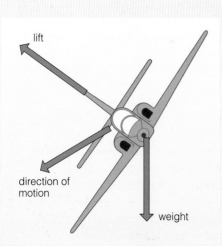

Figure 5.7

Changing the angle between the wing and the airflow changes the lift. The angle is changed by using flaps called elevators at the back of the aeroplane (Figure 5.6). To increase the lift, the elevators are raised. This pushes the back of the aeroplane down, which also pushes the front of the aeroplane up and changes the angle.

On take-off and landing, the size and shape of the wing is increased by flaps which come out of the back of the wing. This increases the area of the wing and the lift at low speeds. When the aeroplane has reached a certain altitude and speed, the flaps are retracted.

A quick way to move downwards is to change the direction of the lift by rolling the aeroplane. The weight will still be directed downwards but the lift will no longer be directed straight upwards, as shown in Figure 5.7.

Wings are shaped so that the air flowing over the top has further to travel than the air flowing under the wing. This creates a low pressure area above the wing and a high pressure area under the wing. The pressure difference provides the required lift, as shown in Figure 5.8.

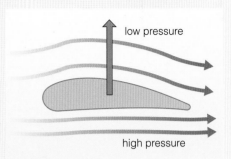

Figure 5.8

Bed of nails

Lying on a bed of nails is not something you should try, but perhaps you could make a small bed of nails and try it out with a balloon. You may need to experiment with how much you blow up the balloon. When the balloon is resting on the nails, several books can be stacked on it before it pops. If the bed of nails is replaced with a single nail, the balloon will pop on contact.

A typical bed of nails is a large wooden table with about 2000 sharp steel nails embedded in it. Due to the equal distribution of body weight over all the nails, the person does not get hurt. A person of mass 70 kg will weigh 700 N and the average weight acting on each nail will be only 0.35 N.

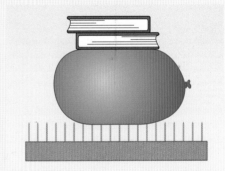

Figure 5.9

Figure 5.10

Car braking system

Look at the car braking system shown in Figure 5.11. A small force on the brake pedal is applied to a small area. This exerts a pressure on the liquid and this pressure is transferred to the pistons in the brakes. These pistons have a large area so that a large force is exerted on the braking disc.

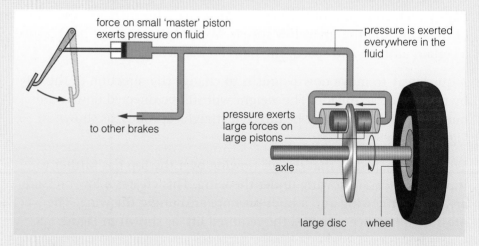

Figure 5.11

Human arm

To hold an object in your hand the moment produced by the load must be balanced by the moment produced by the effort from your muscle. The effort is a lot closer to the pivot than your hand; therefore the muscle needs to provide a force that is much greater than the load.

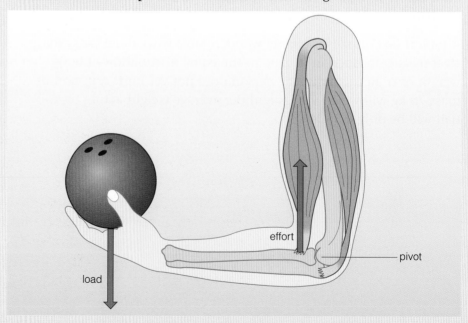

Figure 5.12

Questions

1 a) What are the four main forces acting on an aeroplane? [4]

b) What causes each force? [4]

[Total 8]

2 An aircraft loses height when it slows down, unless it changes the shape of its wings. Explain why this happens. [Total 3]

3 What is happening to an aeroplane if

a) the lift is less than the weight [1]

b) the thrust is greater than the drag? [1]

[Total 2]

4 What effect does the shape of the wings have on the lift? [Total 2]

5 Why can a person lie on a bed of nails without getting hurt? [Total 1]

6 A hydraulic braking system for a car has two pistons, one for the brake pedal and one for the brake blocks. Explain why these pistons are different sizes.

[Total 3]

7 Figure 5.13 shows a human arm supporting a load of 20 N. The load is 32 cm from the pivot. If the effort from the muscle is applied 4 cm from the pivot, what force is the muscle exerting? [Total 4]

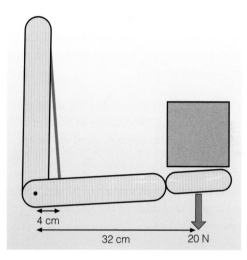

Figure 5.13

End of section questions

1 A cyclist travelled a distance of 80 m in a time of 10 s. Calculate the cyclist's average speed.
[Total 3]

2 Rashid walked from his English room to the physics laboratory at an average speed of 1.5 m/s. The journey took him exactly 2 minutes. Calculate the distance he travelled from the English room to the physics laboratory. *[Total 3]*

3 In July 1985, Steve Cram broke the world mile record by running the distance of 1609 m in 226 s. Calculate his average speed during the race.
[Total 3]

4 A cheetah can run at a speed of 37 m/s. Calculate how long it would take a cheetah to run a distance of 100 m. *[Total 3]*

5 Table 1 shows the distance travelled by a rowing boat during its journey across a lake.

Table 1

Time taken (s)	0	20	40	60	80	100	120	140
Distance travelled (m)	0	20	60	120	180	240	300	360

   a) Plot a distance–time graph for the journey. *[5]*
   b) On your graph, mark the point at which the boat reached maximum speed. *[1]*
   c) Calculate the maximum speed of the boat. *[3]*
   d) Calculate the average speed of the boat *[3]*
   e) Sketch a speed–time graph for the journey. *[2]*
[Total 14]

6 Fiona wrote down her height, mass and weight on a piece of paper (Figure 1).
   a) What is Fiona's mass? *[1]*
   b) How much does Fiona weigh? *[1]*
   c) If Fiona went to the Moon, which of these three values would change? *[1]*
[Total 3]

520 N

1.7 m

52 kg

Figure 1

7 Explain in terms of friction why it would be dangerous to put oil on the brake blocks of a bike.
[Total 3]

8 Figure 2 shows the forces acting on a boat sailing at a steady speed.
   a) What is the name given to force X? *[1]*
   b) What is the value of force X? *[1]*
   c) What is the value of the drag? *[1]*
[Total 3]

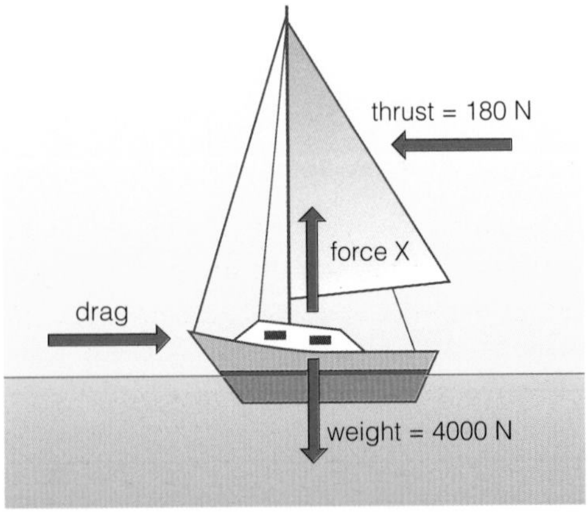

thrust = 180 N

force X

drag

weight = 4000 N

Figure 2

9 Two sets of identical coins were balanced on a ruler and pivot. The first set contained 6 coins positioned 16 cm to the right of the pivot. When the ruler balanced the second set of coins were 8 cm to the left of the pivot.
How many coins were there in the second set? You may need to draw a diagram to help you answer this question. *[Total 3]*

10 Figure 3 shows a load of 10 N being supported by an effort applied to a lever system.
a) Calculate the moment produced by the load. *[3]*
b) What moment is the effort supplying? *[1]*
c) Calculate the value of the effort.
[3]
[Total 7]

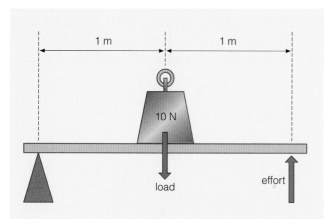

1 m   1 m

10 N

load   effort

Figure 3

11 When using a wheelbarrow to carry a heavy object, why is it better to place the object as close to the front of the wheelbarrow as possible? *[Total 2]*

12 Drawing pins have one end with a large flat surface and the other end has a sharp point. Using the words **force**, **pressure** and **area**, explain why the drawing pin goes into the wall rather than into your thumb when you use it correctly. *[Total 3]*

13 You can lie on a bed of nails without hurting yourself. Why could you not walk on the same bed of nails? *[Total 3]*

14 A computer monitor weighing 160 N rested on a desk. The area of contact between its base and the desk was 800 cm². Calculate the pressure exerted on the desk by the computer monitor. *[Total 3]*

15 Explain why dams need to be very much thicker at the bottom than they are at the top. *[Total 3]*

16 The brake pedal of a hydraulic braking system applies a force of 400 N to an area of 4 cm².
a) Calculate the pressure in the fluid. *[3]*
b) Calculate the force this pressure would exert on a brake piston with an area of 25 cm². *[3]*
[Total 6]

17 A submarine can withstand the high pressures 1300 m deep in water. Airliners, can withstand the low pressures at over 10 000 m up in the atmosphere. Suggest reasons for these differences. *[Total 5]*

18
P Plan an investigation to test how well different shaped objects move through wallpaper paste.

19
P List the variables that could be changed when making a spring.

20
R Find out about the following.
a) A unit of speed called the **knot**.
b) What **mach 2** means.

21
R There are many different kinds of barometer that can be used to measure atmospheric pressure. Carry out some research on barometers and write an information sheet about them.

22
R Find out about the French physicist and mathematician, Blaise Pascal.

5.1 Static electricity

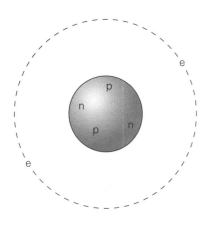

e = electron
p = proton
n = neutron

Figure 1.1 *The structure of a helium atom.*

Why does some clothing crackle when you undress? What causes lightning? Electricity is all around us – static electricity can build up on many objects. It can also make your hair stand on end!

All substances are made up of atoms. An atom consists of **protons** (positively charged particles) and **neutrons** (which have no charge). These particles are in the central **nucleus**. **Electrons** have a negative charge and they orbit the central nucleus.

An atom is electrically neutral. This means that an atom has the same number of positive charges as negative charges. Only the electrons can be moved because they are on the outside of the atom.

When a plastic ruler is rubbed with a dry cloth it will pick up little pieces of paper. What has happened to the plastic ruler to allow it to do this? The ruler is made of atoms and each atom has the same number of electrons and protons in it. It is electrically neutral. When a cloth is rubbed against the ruler friction helps to move some of the electrons. If the electrons are moved from the ruler onto the cloth then the ruler will have fewer electrons. The ruler therefore has a positive charge. The cloth will have extra electrons and it will have an overall negative charge.

?

1 What charge do each of the following have?
a) proton [1]
b) neutron [1]
c) electron [1]
[Total 3]
2 Why can't positive charges be rubbed off a material? [Total 2]

!

The ancient Greeks were the first people to notice the effects of static electricity. The amber beads they wore rubbed against their skin, became charged up, and soon became very dusty.

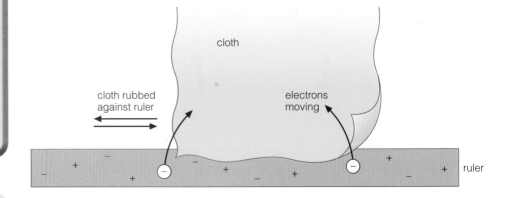

Figure 1.2 *The ruler is being charged up using the cloth.*

Sometimes the electrons will move from the cloth and onto the plastic, depending on the type of materials used. This will give the plastic a negative charge and the cloth a positive charge. Glass can also be charged up in this way. We call this type of charge **static electricity**. Any substance that will allow electricity to flow through it easily cannot be charged with static electricity and is called a **conductor**. Unless insulated, the charge flows away and does not build up. Only an **insulator** can be charged with static electricity this way as electrons cannot flow through the insulator to replace the electrons that have been lost.

If two pieces of acetate, each with a positive charge, are brought close together they will push away from each other or **repel**. If one piece of acetate is replaced with polythene which has a negative charge, they now have different charges and they will pull towards each other or **attract**. They have opposite charges.

Small particles are attracted to objects charged with static electricity. Dust will stick to a charged mirror and small pieces of paper will stick to a charged plastic ruler. When you rub a balloon on your clothes it will also become charged and stick to a wall.

When a charged ruler is brought near a fine stream of water from a tap the stream of water bends towards the ruler. The unlike charges on the water molecules are attracted to the charges on the ruler. This is called an **induced charge**.

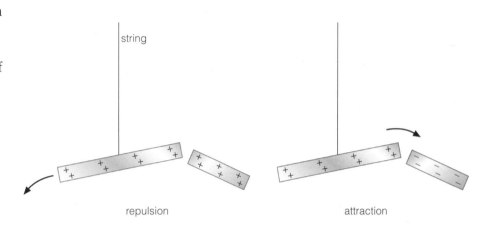

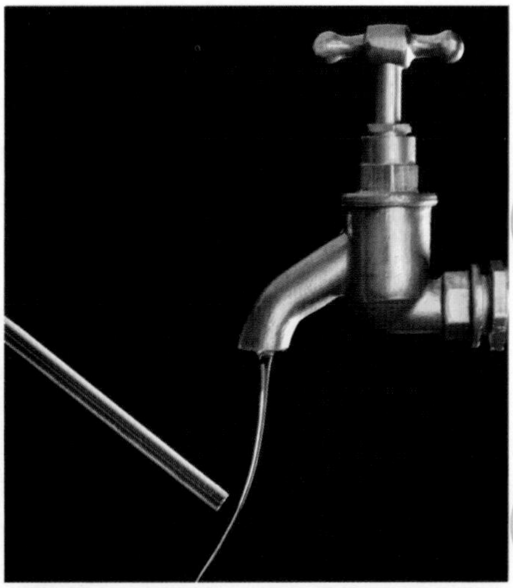

repulsion   attraction

Figure 1.3 *Same charges (or 'like' charges) repel and opposite charges attract.*

Figure 1.4 *The charged rod induces a charge in the water.*

! Like charges repel and opposite charges attract.

? **3** When rubbed, what charge is left on a polythene rod?   [Total 1]

The Van de Graaff generator

In the laboratory we can make static electricity using a Van de Graaff generator. This machine was invented in 1931.

The generator uses friction between the belt and a Perspex roller to charge the belt with a positive charge. This charge is carried by the belt to another roller at the top. Electrons move from the dome to the belt to neutralise the charge so the dome gets a positive charge. The

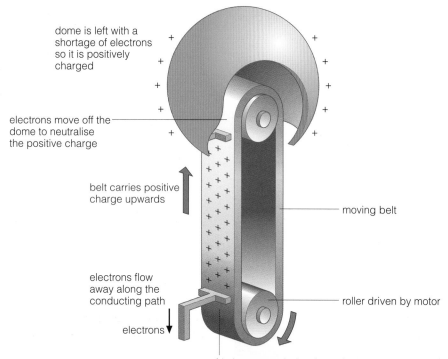

dome is left with a shortage of electrons so it is positively charged

electrons move off the dome to neutralise the positive charge

belt carries positive charge upwards

moving belt

electrons flow away along the conducting path

electrons ▼

roller driven by motor

friction causes belt to lose electrons

Figure 1.5 *How a Van de Graaff generator works.*

belt moves round to become charged up again. This process continues and a high positive charge collects on the dome. If the dome is then earthed a small spark like a small bolt of lightning will be seen. It is possible to charge up a person if you make sure they are not touching earth. If given a chance an electric charge will always go to earth.

Lightning

Inside storm clouds small particles of ice, carried by convection currents, move upward past bigger ones and rub against them as they move. This movement causes the clouds to become charged up. As the cloud passes over the Earth the opposite charge is induced in the ground. If the charge becomes large enough a flash of lightning will occur between the cloud and the Earth or between different clouds.

Lightning can reach temperatures of 30 000°C. There are about 80 lightning flashes per second worldwide.

Figure 1.6

Summary

- An atom consists of protons, neutrons and electrons.
- Some electrons can be moved away from their atoms.
- Conductors cannot be charged with static electricity.
- Like charges repel and opposite charges attract.
- Lightning is a movement of electrons.

Questions

1 An atom is electrically _____. To make an atom charged, _____ have to be added or removed. Unlike charges _____ and _____ charges repel. *[Total 2]*

2 a) Which of the following sentences are correct? *[2]*
   i) A plastic comb with extra electrons will have a positive charge.
   ii) Two charges that are the same as each other will repel.
   iii) A metal rod is easy to charge with static electricity.
   iv) In an atom only electrons can be moved from place to place.
   v) Protons have a negative charge.

   b) For each statement that is incorrect, say what is wrong. Re-write the statement to make it correct. *[3]*
   [Total 5]

3 If a balloon is rubbed on a jumper the balloon will charge up with a negative charge.
   a) Explain how the balloon becomes charged. *[2]*
   b) Will the jumper also have a charge? *[1]*
   c) If so, what charge will it have and why? *[2]*
   [Total 5]

4 When cling film is pulled from a roll it will stick to your hand. Why does it do this? *[Total 3]*

5 Metal car doors can be painted with charged powder paint. This works better if the car door is earthed.
   a) How does this work? *[2]*
   b) What are the advantages of using charged powder paint? *[2]*
   [Total 4]

6 A charged plastic pen will have an effect on a small trickle of water. What will happen to the water and why? *[Total 3]*

7 How could you change the construction of a Van der Graff generator so the dome becomes negatively charged? *[Total 3]*

8 Why does some clothing crackle when you undress? *[Total 3]*

9 Why do some lightning strikes hit other clouds instead of the ground? *[Total 3]*

5.2 Simple electric circuits

What is an electric current and how is it measured? With some Christmas tree lights when one bulb blows they all go out. With others it is easy to see the one that has broken. This is because circuits can be set up in series or parallel.

An electric current is a flow of electrons from one place to another. Electricity will flow through metals because the atoms of the metals are surrounded by electrons that are free to move. The movement or flow of these electrons is called an electric current.

A simple circuit

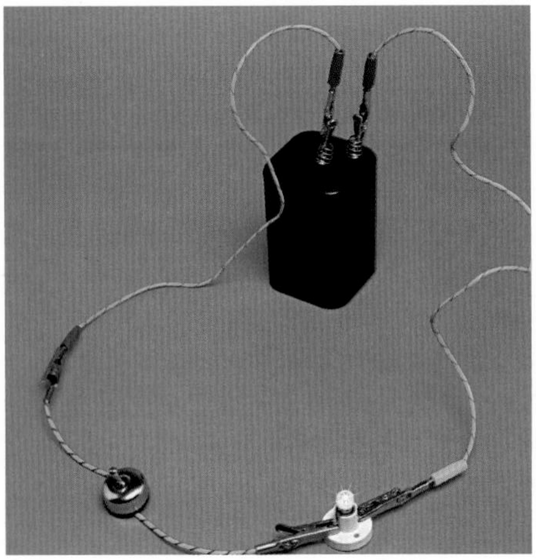

If you want a bulb to light you will need a cell, some connecting wires and a switch. When all these are connected together you have a complete **circuit** and the bulbs light.

When the switch is closed the electrons will move through the wires from the negative end of the cell, through the bulb and back to the positive end. You have given the electrons a path to move along (wires), and energy from the cell to move. The chemical reaction in the cell pushes the electrons round the circuit (like water through a pipe). It is more difficult for the electrons to move through the thin wires in the bulb and some of their energy is transferred to heat and light. The process will only stop when the cell runs out of chemical energy. The electrons will then no longer move because there is nothing to push them around the circuit.

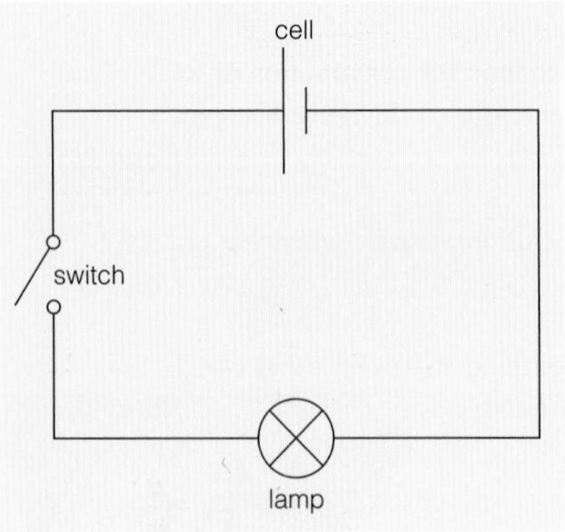

In science we have a way of drawing circuits quickly and accurately by using symbols for all the parts of the circuit. The circuit does not need labels. Figure 2.2 shows the circuit in Figure 2.1 as a circuit diagram.

Conventional current and electron flow

An electric current is a flow of electrons going through all parts of the circuit. The electrons have a negative charge and are pushed from the negative terminal of the cell. They are attracted round the circuit to the positive terminal. When experiments were first carried out with electricity, scientists did not know about electrons. They agreed to talk about electricity going from positive to negative. We call this **conventional current**. We now know that this is incorrect. The movement of the electrons is the **electron flow**.

Figure 2.1 *A simple circuit.*

Figure 2.2 *A circuit diagram of the simple circuit shown in Figure 2.1.*

The electrons have to work very hard to go through a bulb. If you give them an easier route they will take it instead. This easier route is called a **short circuit**. Sometimes the route may be longer but it is always easier.

Series and parallel circuits

Series circuit

In the circuit shown in Figure 2.4, the bulbs and the cell are placed in one loop. They are in a **series circuit**. If there is a break in the circuit the electrons cannot go through the wires and no current flows. The more bulbs that are added to the circuit then the dimmer each bulb will be. This is because it is more difficult for the electrons to flow round the circuit. If you add more cells in series the bulbs will become brighter.

If Christmas tree lights are in series and one bulb breaks, all the bulbs go out because the circuit is broken. It is very difficult to find the broken bulb.

Parallel circuit

In this circuit there is more than one possible path for the current to flow round. This is a **parallel circuit**. The current gets to a junction and splits up to go through each branch. This means if one bulb is broken the others will still work because there is still a complete circuit for the electrons to flow round. The current can still go through the other bulbs. Adding more bulbs to the same circuit does not affect the brightness of the other bulbs. Cells can also be put in parallel to each other. This will not make the bulbs any brighter but the circuit will work for longer.

When Christmas tree lights are in a parallel circuit, it is much easier to find a broken bulb because the rest of the bulbs still work.

Resistance

All the parts of a circuit will try to stop the electrons from going through them. The parts try to resist the flow of electrons. This is called **resistance**. Some metals, like copper, have a lower resistance than other metals and we say they are good conductors. The resistance of a wire depends on its length, its material and gauge (thickness). The more difficult it is for the electrons to get through the wire, the larger the resistance of the wire. A long thin wire would be very difficult for

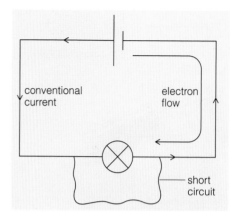

Figure 2.3 *The circuit shows the way the electrons are flowing and the direction of the conventional current. The wire added to the circuit is showing a short circuit.*

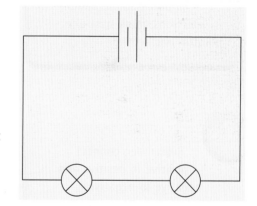

Figure 2.4 *A series circuit.*

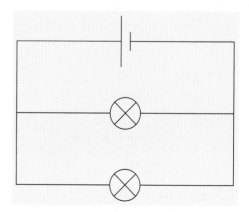

Figure 2.5 *A parallel circuit.*

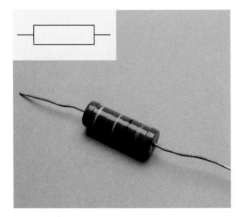

Figure 2.6 *A resistor and its symbol.*

electrons to pass through. Therefore it has a high resistance to the flow of current. Resistance has the symbol R and is measured in **ohms** (Ω).

Measuring an electric current

You can see how much electricity is flowing in a circuit by the brightness of the bulbs. This is not a very reliable method. Electricity is the flow of electrons through the wires. A larger current means that there are more electrons flowing. An instrument that will 'count' these electrons will measure the current. This instrument is called an **ammeter**.

An ammeter should have a low resistance so that it does not affect the current in the circuit. An ammeter must be connected in series in a circuit, so that all the electrons will go through it. Current is measured in amperes, usually shortened to amps or A. Current has the symbol I.

An ammeter must be connected the correct way round in a circuit with the positive terminals of the meter and the cell connected.

You can use an ammeter to measure the current in any part of a series or parallel circuit.

If you put an ammeter in different positions in a series circuit as shown in Figure 2.7a all the readings will be identical. The number of electrons going through the wires remains constant.

If the readings are taken in a parallel circuit as shown in Figure 2.7b they will not be the same as each other. The current splits and travels through the different branches. The current in all the branches adds up to the current coming from the cell.

> One amp is about 6 million, million, million electrons going past one point in one second.

> Remember, connect positive to positive and negative to negative.

No current is used up in a series or parallel circuit since you always end up with the same ammeter reading on each side of the cells. So if current is not used up why do cells eventually stop working? The electrons need energy to move through the wires. This energy comes from chemical energy in the cells. When this chemical energy runs out the electrons will no longer be pushed around the wires and so no current flows.

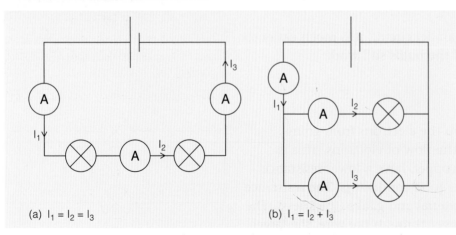

(a) $I_1 = I_2 = I_3$

(b) $I_1 = I_2 + I_3$

Figure 2.7 *Measuring current in a) series and b) parallel circuits.*

The electrons use up most energy when they do the most work, e.g. moving through a bulb. We can measure this energy difference called potential difference (PD) using a **voltmeter**. It is also possible to measure the electrical 'push' of a cell, the electromotive force (EMF), with a voltmeter.

Measuring PD and EMF

A voltmeter is connected in parallel across the component or cell being measured. The current should flow through the circuit and not the meter so a voltmeter must have a high resistance to current. A voltmeter is connected with the positive terminal of the meter to the positive side of the circuit (see rules for an ammeter). EMF and PD are measured in volts and written as the symbol V.

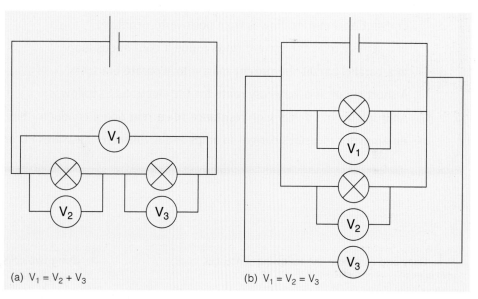

(a) $V_1 = V_2 + V_3$ (b) $V_1 = V_2 = V_3$

Figure 2.8 *Measuring the PD in a) series and b) parallel circuits.*

A voltmeter is connected across different components in a series circuit as shown in Figure 2.8a and readings are taken. The voltages across each individual component add up to the voltage across all the components. In this case:

$$V_1 = V_2 + V_3$$

If readings are taken in a parallel circuit as shown in Figure 2.8b then all the readings should be identical to each other.

An electric eel generates up to 650 V and stuns its prey as the current passes from its head to its tail. It also uses a weak electric field to navigate.

Summary

- A flow of current is the movement of electrical charge, usually electrons.
- Electrons move from the negative terminal of a cell to the positive terminal of a cell.
- Conventional current flow is from positive to negative.
- In a series circuit the current flows round a continuous loop.
- In a parallel circuit the current splits into separate branches.
- A short circuit is a very easy route for the electrons to follow.
- An insulator has a very high resistance to current and a conductor has a low resistance to current.
- An ammeter measures current in amps and a voltmeter measures PD and EMF in volts.

Questions

1 Copy and complete the following sentences.

An electric current is a flow of _____. For this to happen there must be a complete _____. Current flows easily through a _____ but it does not flow easily through an _____. An _____ measures current and must be placed in _____ in a circuit. A voltmeter measures _____ and must be placed in _____ in a circuit.

[Total 4]

2 Match the symbols shown in Figure 2.9 to their names.
ammeter
voltmeter
wire
cell
bulb
switch   [Total 4]

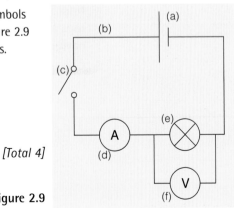

Figure 2.9

3 Using two cells and three bulbs draw circuit diagrams to:
a) make the three bulbs as bright as possible   [1]
b) make the three bulbs as dim as possible   [1]
c) control one bulb only by adding a switch.   [1]

[Total 3]

4 Using one cell, one bulb and one switch, draw a circuit diagram to show the bulb working only when the switch is NOT closed.   [Total 3]

5 There are three living areas in a tent. Each area needs a light, which can be controlled from that area. You only have one large cell.
a) Draw a circuit diagram to show the lighting for the tent.   [3]
b) How many bulbs and switches will you need?   [1]

[Total 4]

5.3 Other circuit components

Streetlights come on when it goes dark. What triggers this action? How does a dimmer switch work?

In the last subsection we looked at basic circuits. There are many types of component used in a circuit. Each one does a different job.

Diodes

A **diode** will only allow current to flow in one direction. The direction that the diode will allow conventional current to flow is indicated by the arrow. The end with the band must be connected to the negative side of the circuit. On the symbol for a diode the straight line is the side where the band is. A diode can be used to protect computers, which would be damaged if the power supply was connected the wrong way round.

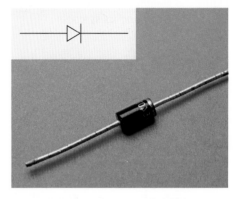

Figure 3.1 *A diode and its symbol.*

Light emitting diode (LED)

Figure 3.2 *A light emitting diode (LED) and its symbol.*

An **LED** is more efficient than a bulb and is sometimes used in circuits instead of a bulb. It allows electricity to flow in one direction only. The LED does not produce light in the same way as a bulb. In this component the electrons in the material move inside the atom when a current flows, releasing energy as they move. Some of this energy we see as light. The most common colour for the LED light is red. If different materials are used they can produce green and yellow light. An LED changes electrical energy to light energy. LEDs only need a small current and will last longer than a bulb.

1 How are the symbols for a diode and an LED different? *[Total 2]*

Light dependent resistor (LDR)

An **LDR** is made up of a piece of semiconducting material joined to two pieces of metal. A semiconductor will allow some current to flow.

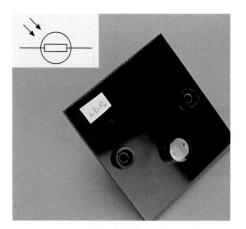

Figure 3.3 *A light dependent resistor (LDR) and its symbol.*

2 Why do rheostats and LDRs both have a rectangle in their circuit symbols? [Total 1]

Its resistance is in-between a conductor and an insulator. The semiconductor has only a few free electrons so a current will not pass through it easily. When light energy falls on the LDR more electrons are released from their atoms and the material will then become a better conductor. When the light energy is removed the LDR goes back to its original state. LDRs are used to ensure streetlights come on when it starts to go dark. They are activated as it goes dark.

Variable resistor (rheostat)

A **variable resistor** can be used to control the size of a current by altering the resistance. Moving the slider controls the length of wire the current must flow through. The longer the wire the lower the current.

In your house you may have a dimmer switch which will allow you to control the brightness of the lights. These are small rheostats. Turning the switch changes the length of wire in contact with the pointer.

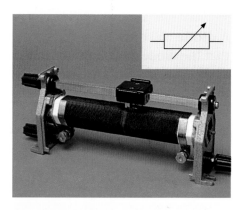

Figure 3.4 *A rheostat and its symbol.*

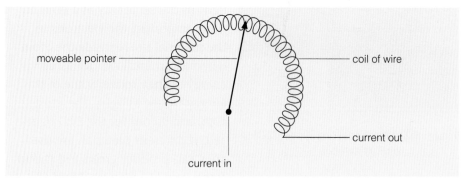

moveable pointer — coil of wire
current in
current out

Figure 3.5 *A dimmer switch.*

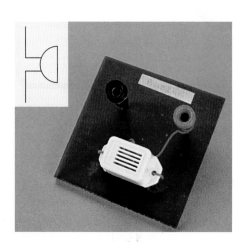

Figure 3.6 *A buzzer and its circuit symbol.*

Buzzer

When an electric current is passed through a buzzer it will vibrate and make a sound. Its can be used in circuits which need to give an audible warning.

Logic gates

Logic gates are part of electronic circuits. They allow a variety of inputs and outputs to be used to control circuits.

AND gate

The symbol for an **AND gate** is shown in Figure 3.7. To explain how it works look at the simple circuit shown in Figure 3.8.

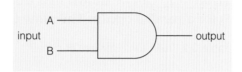

Figure 3.7 *The symbol for an AND gate.*

For the bulb to light, switches A and B must be closed. The current cannot flow until both switches are closed. This is like an AND gate where there must be an input to both A and B for the gate to respond. A microwave oven makes use of an AND gate. It will only work if the door is closed AND the on switch is pressed.

The outputs for the different states of the series circuit shown in Figure 3.8 can be shown in a truth table, as shown in Table 3.1. This is for a series circuit. The same table applies for an AND gate.

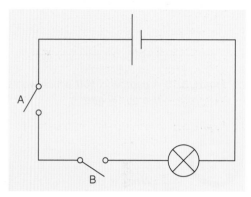

Figure 3.8 *A series circuit which works like an AND gate.*

Table 3.1 *Truth table for an AND circuit.*

Switch A	Switch B	Bulb
Open	Open	Off
Closed	Open	Off
Open	Closed	Off
Closed	Closed	On

OR gate

The symbol for an **OR gate** is shown in Figure 3.9. To explain how it works look at the simple circuit shown in Figure 3.10.

For the bulb to light, switch A or switch B can be closed, which allows the current to flow. This is like an OR gate where there must be an input to A or B for the gate to respond. Heating systems in houses

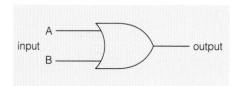

Figure 3.9 *The symbol for an OR gate.*

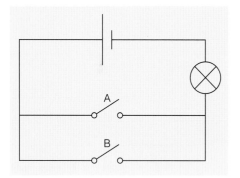

Figure 3.10 *A parallel circuit which works like an OR gate.*

? 3 What is the difference between Tables 3.1 and 3.2? [Total 1]
4 What is the difference between an AND gate and an OR gate? [Total 2]

make use of OR gates. For example, a hot water heater may have a time switch which turns on the heater at certain times of day. There will also be a manual switch if you want to heat water at other times. Either switch can be used to turn the hot water heater on.

The outputs for the different states of the series circuit shown in Figure 3.10 can be shown in a truth table, as shown in Table 3.2. This is for a parallel circuit. The same table applies for an OR gate.

Table 3.2 *Truth table for an OR circuit.*

Switch A	Switch B	Bulb
Open	Open	Off
Closed	Open	On
Open	Closed	On
Closed	Closed	On

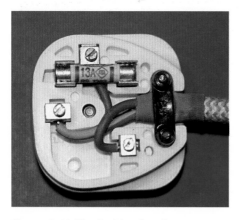

Figure 3.11 *The inside of a plug.*

Using electricity safely

Mains electricity is dangerous and could kill you if you touch a bare wire carrying a current. Wires are covered in an insulating material, usually plastic. Plugs and sockets are also insulated with plastic cases. Water is a good conductor of electricity so it is important not to touch plugs and switches with wet hands. Never use plugs that are broken or have loose wires.

If too high a current flows through an electrical appliance it might be damaged. Using the correct fuse can protect appliances. Fuses can be found in plugs and sometimes in the appliance itself. A fuse is a piece of wire with a low melting point placed in the live part of the circuit.

In a plug the current flows through the live wire (brown). The current flows through the fuse first. If there is a surge of current the fuse will get hot and melt. The fuse 'blows' and the current can no longer flow.

It is important that the correct fuse is fitted in a plug. The fuse should let enough current through so the appliance will work but 'blow' if there is too much. The most common fuses are rated at 3 A, 5 A and

13 A. If an appliance has a heating element in it, it will need a 13 A fuse. This is a simple rule to work out the correct fuse to use.

The National Grid

Power stations produce electricity and it is transmitted around the country by cables called power lines. This network of power lines is called the National Grid. Electricity has to flow along miles of wire before it reaches people's homes. The current heats up the wire and some electrical energy is wasted as heat. If the electricity is transmitted at high voltages and low currents, less energy is wasted.

It would be too dangerous to have very high voltages in our homes. This means that the voltage of the electricity must be increased as it leaves the power station and decreased before it comes into our homes. A transformer is used to change the voltage. There are two types of transformer. A step-up transformer increases voltage (for example between power station and power lines). A step-down transformer decreases voltage (for example from the power lines to homes).

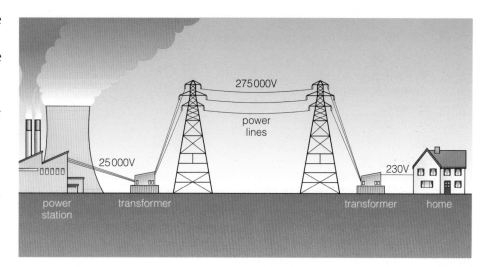

Figure 3.12

Summary

- ⊙ A diode is like a one way valve, allowing current to flow in one direction.
- ⊙ A light emitting diode uses a smaller current than a bulb and gives off (emits) light.
- ⊙ A light dependent resistor uses light as a trigger and works like a switch.
- ⊙ You can alter the size of the current in a circuit by altering the resistance of the circuit – higher resistance means a lower current.
- ⊙ Electricity is dangerous and it is important that electrical devices have the correct fuses and properly wired plugs.

Questions

1 Copy and complete the following sentences.
In a rheostat the resistance can be _____ .
A diode will allow a current to flow in _____
direction. When light shines on a LDR _____
electrons are released. The higher the resistance of a
wire the _____ the current. In an AND gate
both _____ must be on to get an output. In
an _____ gate only one input must be on to
get an output. *[Total 3]*

2 Draw the symbols for the following components:
a) LED [1]
b) diode [1]
c) variable resistor [1]
d) buzzer [1]
e) OR gate. [1]
[Total 5]

3 Look at the circuit diagram shown in Figure 3.13. This
is a circuit for a hairdryer. Which switches must be
closed for:
a) cold air to be blown out [1]
b) warm air to be blown out? [1]
c) This circuit allows a possibly dangerous situation
where the hairdryer heats without blowing air. How
could you change it to make it safe? [2]
[Total 4]

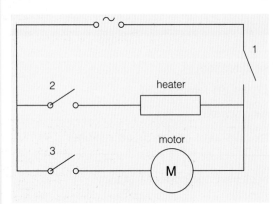

Figure 3.13 *The circuit for a hairdryer.*

4 What do the following abbreviations stand for?
a) LED [1]
b) LDR [1]
[Total 2]

5 Look at Figure 3.14.
a) Will the bulb light up? [1]
b) What will happen if the cell is reversed? [1]
[Total 2]

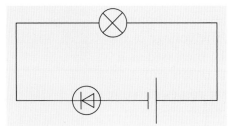

Figure 3.14

6 Design a leaflet to point out some of the hazards
associated with using electricity in the home.
[Total 4]

7 a) What does a transformer do? [1]
b) Why are transformers needed in the National
Grid? [4]
[Total 5]

8 Look at the circuit shown in Figure 3.15. Draw up a
truth table for this circuit, which will show the result
for every combination of the three switches. *[Total 4]*

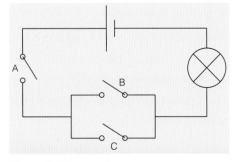

Figure 3.15

5.4 Magnetism

How does a compass work? **Magnets** are everywhere, but only some substances are magnetic.

A form of magnetic rock called lodestone has been known about for a long time. It was used to make the first compasses. Lodestone, or magnetite as it is now called, can still be found. Three elements, iron, cobalt and nickel, are magnetic and are called ferromagnetic materials. Steel also has magnetic properties because of the iron in it.

Close to each end of a magnet is an area called a magnetic pole. If a magnet is suspended on a piece of thread it will turn until one pole points north. This is called the north-seeking pole or north pole. The end pointing south is the south-seeking pole or south pole. When two north poles are put together they push each other away or repel. A north and south pole will pull each other together or attract.

Like poles repel and opposite poles attract.

A piece of iron will be attracted to a magnet but the iron is not a magnet because the iron and the magnet will not repel each other. If two metals repel they must have magnetic poles and so they must both be magnets.

What makes iron magnetic?

To answer this question we need to look inside the metal at the atoms that it is made from. Inside a piece of iron each atom acts as a small magnet called a dipole. They are grouped together in **domains**. Domains in an unmagnetised piece of iron are arranged in random directions and their effects cancel each other out.

A magnet will attract the iron but the iron itself is not a magnet. When the iron is exposed to a magnetic field, the domains line up in the magnetic field. All the north poles point in the same direction.

When all the domains are lined up the magnet cannot get any stronger. It is a saturated magnet. If you cut a magnet in half you will have two magnets. Each magnet will have its own north and south pole.

Iron is called a soft magnetic material. It is an easy metal to magnetise but it loses the magnetism very quickly. Steel is difficult to magnetise but once magnetised it keeps it. Steel is called a hard magnetic material.

> ❗ The brain cells of some birds have been found to contain magnetite. This may be sensitive to the Earth's magnetic field and help them to navigate.

> ❗ The only way to test if two materials are magnets is to see if they will repel each other.

piece of iron

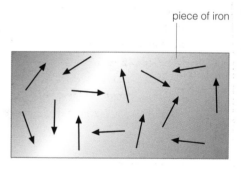

Figure 4.1 *An unmagnetised piece of iron.*

magnet

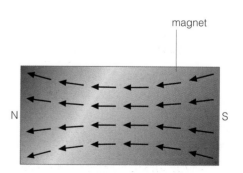

Figure 4.2 *Magnetic domains inside a magnet.*

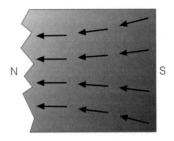

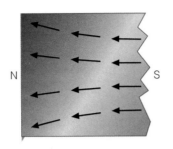

Steel is used to make permanent magnets and iron is used to make temporary magnets.

Figure 4.3 *A magnet broken in half forms two magnets.*

Destroying magnetism

If the domains in a magnet are given energy to move they will revert back to a random arrangement. Some of the magnetism will be lost. You can destroy a magnet by heating it, dropping it or generally being rough with it. Each time a magnet is heated or dropped more domains will become arranged in random directions and the magnet will become weaker.

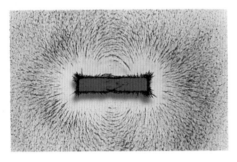

Figure 4.4 *The magnetic field round a bar magnet.*

The magnetic field

When two strong magnets are put close together you can feel the force between them before they touch. The space around a magnet where it can affect magnetic materials is called the **magnetic field**. You can show the field by using iron filings or plotting compasses. The lines shown by the iron filings never cross each other and are concentrated around the poles. The poles of a magnet are not at the ends of the magnet but a small distance in from each end.

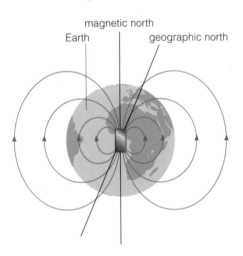

Figure 4.5 *The Earth's magnetic field.*

The Earth's magnetic field

The structure of the centre of the Earth makes the Earth act as if it has a large bar magnet inside it. The magnetic north pole is not in the same place as the geographic north pole. In fact the magnetic north pole moves slightly each year. Over long periods of time (thousands of years) it reverses. The north pole of a magnet will point to magnetic north but two north poles will repel.

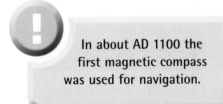

In about AD 1100 the first magnetic compass was used for navigation.

Summary

- A magnet has a north pole and a south pole.
- Like poles repel and opposite poles attract.
- Iron will make a temporary magnet.
- Steel will make a permanent magnet.
- The north pole of a magnet is really a north-seeking pole.
- The Earth has a magnetic field.

Questions

1 Copy and complete the following sentences. A magnet has a north pole and a _____ pole. The pole that points to magnetic north is called a north-_____ pole. When two north poles are put together they _____. Around a magnet there is a magnetic _____. Iron makes a _____ magnet. A permanent magnet is made from _____. Other magnetic materials are _____ and _____. *[Total 4]*

2 You have found three metal bars all painted white. One bar is a magnet, one is made from copper and one is a piece of iron. Using nothing else how can you find out which is which? *[Total 4]*

3 Magnets can be used to hold a refrigerator door closed. Write down five other places where you might find a magnet in use. *[Total 5]*

4 The Earth acts like a giant magnet. People can use this magnetic field to find their way around. Describe one way the Earth's magnetic field can be used for navigation. *[Total 2]*

5 How could you use magnetism to sort cans for recycling? Most cans are made from aluminium or steel. *[Total 2]*

6 Explain why a compass needle always points to magnetic north. *[Total 2]*

7 a) Copy the diagram of the two magnets shown in Figure 4.6. Draw the magnetic field between the magnets. *[2]*

b) Repeat the diagram but this time turn one of the magnets round the other way. *[2]*
[Total 4]

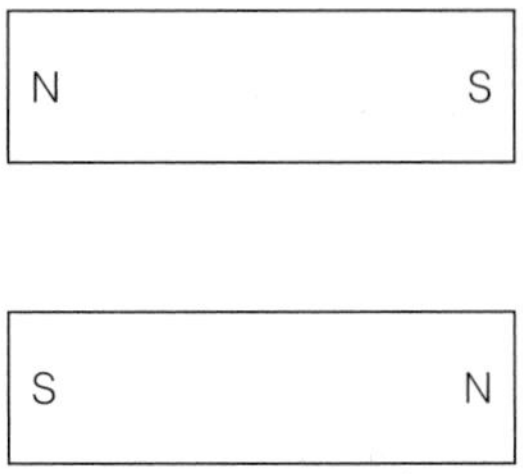

| N | S |

| S | N |

Figure 4.6

5.5 Electricity and magnetism

What is the connection between doorbells, relays and magnetism? Any wire carrying an electric current will have a magnetic field round it. The current flowing through the wire generates the magnetic field.

The magnetic field around a straight conductor

The magnetic field around a conductor can be shown with iron filings or a plotting compass.

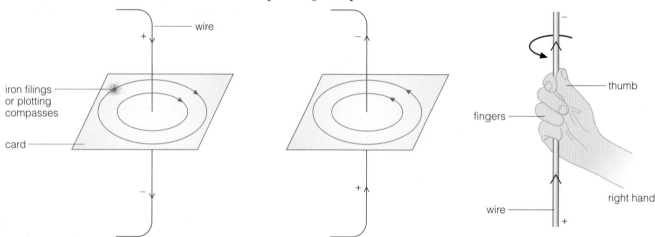

Figure 5.1 *The magnetic field round a straight conductor.*

Figure 5.2 *The right-hand grip rule.*

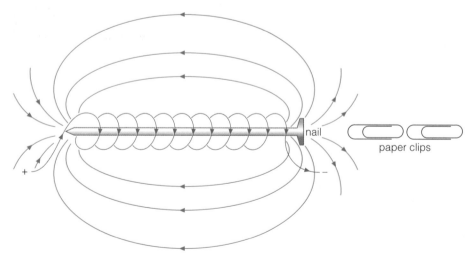

Figure 5.3 *The magnetic field round a coil.*

The magnetic field forms circles around the wire. The direction of the field depends on the direction of the conventional current. An easy way to remember the direction is to imagine holding the wire in your *right* hand and pointing your thumb in the direction of the current. The magnetic field follows the direction of your fingers.

A coil of wire produces a magnetic field similar to that of a bar magnet. An iron nail placed in the centre of the coil will become magnetised. The nail will then attract paper clips as shown in Figure 5.3. Iron is a soft magnetic material. It will only be a magnet while the current is flowing.

Electricity and magnetism

Turn the current off and the iron will lose its magnetism. This device is called an **electromagnet**. It is a magnet that can be turned on and off.

You can make a permanent magnet by replacing the iron with steel. Steel keeps its magnetism.

How can electro-magnets be useful?

Look at Figure 5.4 and try to work out where the current flows when the switch is pushed. The coil becomes an electromagnet and attracts the armature towards it. The hammer hits the bell. At the same time a gap is made between the springy metal strip and the contact screw. The current cannot flow so the coil is no longer an electromagnet. The armature springs back to its original position and contact is made again. The current can flow and the whole process starts again. This continues until you take your finger off the switch. The hammer will hit the bell several times a second.

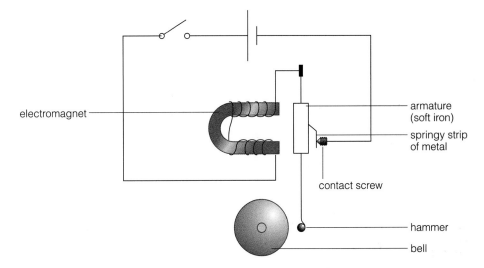

Figure 5.4 *An electric bell.*

The relay

A relay is a magnetic switch. It uses a small current to switch on a larger one. Figure 5.5 shows the relay system used to turn the starter

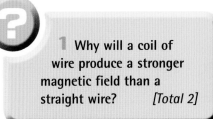

1 Why will a coil of wire produce a stronger magnetic field than a straight wire? *[Total 2]*

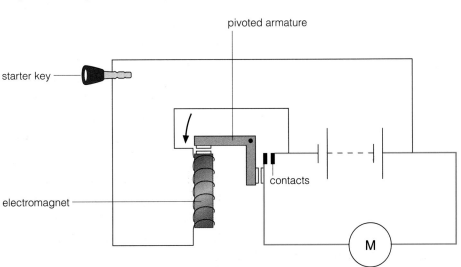

Figure 5.5 *The relay system used in starting a car.*

2 Write down another use where a relay switch could help. [Total 1]

motor of a car. The starter motor needs a large current, which needs to be carried by thick wires. A relay is used to keep these wires as short as possible. It also means that there is only a small current flowing through the circuit with the starter key in it. This makes the circuit safer. A small current from the ignition magnetises an electromagnet. This attracts the iron armature, closing the contacts. A large current will now turn the starter motor.

Reed switch

Reed relays are used for door switches in burglar alarms.

A **reed switch** is operated with a magnet. Inside the glass bulb are two strips made of magnetic material a small distance apart. The magnetic material is usually iron. When a magnet is brought close to the switch the strips of metal become magnetised and are attracted to each other. When the magnet is moved away they lose their magnetism. The metal is springy so they move apart.

In electronics a reed switch can operate as a **reed relay**. The switch is placed inside a coil of wire. When a current flows in the coil it acts as a magnet, activating the switch.

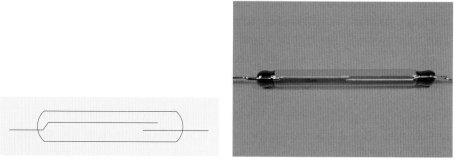

Figure 5.6 *A reed switch and its symbol.*

Summary

- When a current goes through a wire a magnetic field is produced around it.
- Any wire carrying an electric current will have a magnetic field around it.
- A coil of wire produces a magnetic field similar to the field of a bar magnet.
- An electromagnet is made by putting a piece of iron inside a coil which has a current flowing through it.
- A relay is a magnetic switch.

Questions

1 Copy and complete the following sentences.
A magnetic field is produced when a current flows _____ a wire. When a piece of iron is placed in the coil it is called an _____. The iron is a magnet when the current is turned _____.
To make a permanent magnet the iron is replaced with _____. *[Total 2]*

2 Which metal would you choose for the centre of an electromagnet? Give one reason for choosing this metal. *[Total 2]*

3 Look at Figure 5.7.
a) Which metal is end A of the barrier made from? *[1]*
b) What happens to the barrier when the electricity is turned on? *[2]*
c) How could you get the barrier to go back down? *[3]*
[Total 6]

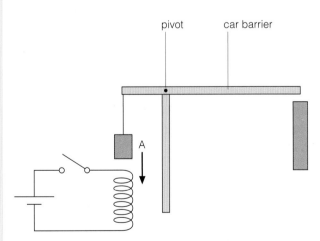

Figure 5.7 *An automatic car barrier.*

4 Read the following sentences and then write them out in the correct order to describe how an electric bell works.
a) The armature is pulled towards the electromagnet and the hammer hits the bell.
b) When the switch is closed the circuit is completed.
c) The armature returns, completing the circuit.
d) The electromagnet is switched on.
e) The current does not flow so the electromagnet does not work.
f) The whole sequence starts again. *[Total 5]*

5 a) Which of the following statements about electromagnets are true? *[2]*
   i) Using more coils of wire will increase the strength of an electromagnet.
   ii) Using copper in the centre of the coil will make the magnet stronger.
   iii) Making the coil narrower will increase the strength of the magnetic field.
   iv) Increasing the current will increase the strength of the magnetic field.
   v) A steel core will make an electromagnet.
b) For each statement that is incorrect, say what is wrong. Re-write the statement to make it correct. *[3]*
[Total 5]

6 Why will the right-hand grip rule only work correctly using your right hand? *[Total 2]*

7 Redraw Figure 5.5 without the pivoted armature, but add in a reed switch, so that the circuits would still function in the same way. *[Total 2]*

5 Electricity and magnetism

Figure 6.1 *If you rub a piece of amber, the amber will attract dust, hair and pieces of paper. It is producing static electricity.*

Figure 6.2 *The Leyden jar stored enough static charge to kill a small animal.*

?

1 Explain what must be happening for a rubbed piece of amber to attract dust. **[Total 2]**

2 The unit for an amount of charge is called the coulomb (C). Why do you think scientists chose this name? **[Total 1]**

Using static electricity

The discovery of static electricity

Static electricity has been known about for thousands of years. Otto von Guericke (1602–1686) was a German diplomat, engineer and mayor of the town of Magdeburg. He invented a static electricity machine made of a large ball of sulphur which rotated while rubbing against a cloth.

In the eighteenth century, Pieter van Musschenbroek invented the Leyden jar. This was a glass jar coated with metal inside and out. A metal rod was pushed into the jar and when it was connected to a static machine, it could store charge.

In America, Benjamin Franklin (1706–1790) was investigating lightning and trying to capture the electricity produced by a flash of lightning in a Leyden jar. He was very lucky that he did not electrocute himself! In the eighteenth century, demonstrating the effects of static electricity was a popular pastime, and scientists made many discoveries as a result of their experiments. For example Charles Coulomb (1736–1806), a French army engineer, built a very sensitive instrument that could measure the strength of the force between two charged objects.

Today we have many uses for static electricity, most of which involve tiny particles. This is because small particles are easily charged and their small mass means they are easily attracted or repelled by charged objects. For example, a photocopier uses a scan of the image to be copied to produce a pattern of charge which then attracts tiny particles of ink and makes them stick to the paper in the same pattern as the original image.

Cleaning air pollution

An **electrostatic precipitator** is often installed in industrial chimneys to clean the smoke that escapes from them. Small particles of soot rising in the smoke pass a grid of charged wires and gain a negative charge. Higher up the chimney, they are attracted to large positively charged collector plates. The electric charges are occasionally switched off and the plates tapped to knock off all the soot. The soot can be collected and disposed of. The electrostatic precipitator cleans smoke of dust and ash particles but cannot remove polluting gases like carbon dioxide.

The negatively charged dust particles are attracted to the positively charged plates and stick to them.

The plates are tapped occasionaly to make the dust fall into the hoppers.

Dust particles collect negative charges as they flow past the wires.

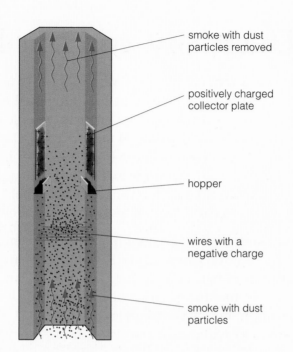

smoke with dust particles removed

positively charged collector plate

hopper

wires with a negative charge

smoke with dust particles

Figure 6.3 *An electrostatic precipitator cleans smoke of dust and ash particles.*

Spray painting

Spray painting car bodies and bicycle frames is much more efficient using static electricity. The metal bicycle frame is connected to a source of negative charge. As the paint is sprayed from the paint gun nozzle, it is given a positive charge. All the paint droplets therefore have a positive charge and so repel each other. This spreads the paint into a large cloud. The positive paint droplets are attracted to the negative bike frame, so they stick onto it. This type of spray painting is very efficient because the paint sticks more strongly than if the particles were not charged, the paint is pulled into all the hard-to-reach nooks and crannies in the frame, and it covers the frame evenly. The other advantage is that little paint misses the frame, so reducing waste.

3 Name two uses of static electricity. *[Total 2]*

4 Why do the uses of static electricity involve small particles? *[Total 2]*

Figure 6.4 *Electrostatic spray painting saves on wasted paint and makes a stronger, more even paint finish on bikes and car bodies.*

5 a) How can electrostatic repulsion be used in spray painting? *[2]*

b) How can electrostatic attraction be used in spray painting? *[2]*
[Total 4]

Questions

1 Why does spray painting a bike frame using electrostatics reduce paint wastage? *[Total 3]*

2 A household air purifier is advertised as being able to remove pollen particles from the air to help hayfever sufferers. Explain how it might work. *[Total 7]*

Electricity and our lives

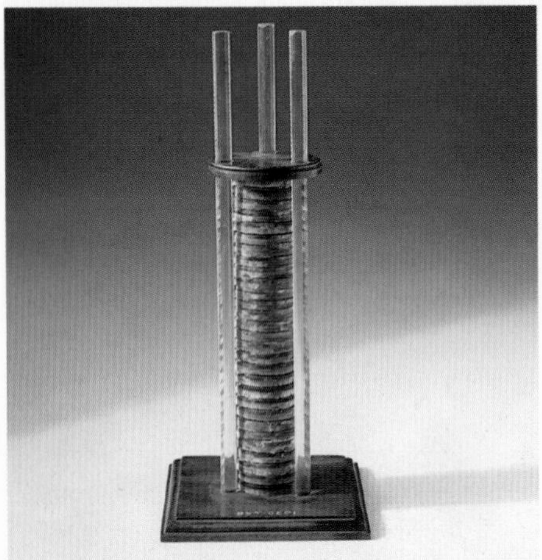

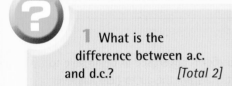

Luigi Galvani (1737–1798) was a lecturer of anatomy at the University of Bologna, Italy. He became very interested in how nerves and muscles work and tried to link electricity with muscle contraction by using a static electricity machine to make the muscles in a frog's leg twitch. He noticed that when he hung frogs' legs from iron railings with a copper hook, the legs began to twitch without any input of electricity. He decided from these observations that animals' bodies contained a new form of electricity, which he called 'animal electricity'.

Alessandro Volta was born in Como, Italy and became a professor of physics at the University of Pavia. Volta heard about Galvani's discoveries but thought that Galvani's explanation was wrong. Volta thought that the electricity had been made by the two metals copper and iron, not by the frog's leg. He tested this theory by making electricity without animal tissue, using the two different metals.

Volta created the first electric cell in 1799, called the **voltaic pile**, using what he had learnt from both his and Galvani's observations. The cell contained the metals zinc and silver. His paper describing the voltaic pile was published in England in 1800 and created great interest. Soon everyone was building voltaic piles (electric cells) and using the steady current they produced to discover new effects. Volta thought you could use the cell to reanimate the dead and did lots of experiments on the bodies of hanged criminals. These experiments gave Mary Shelley the idea for her novel, *Frankenstein*.

Volta and Galvani were both partly right. Volta was right to suggest that different metals cause the electricity. We now also know that nerves in animal bodies carry electrical impulses (although electricity does not travel through nerves in the same way as it travels through wires). This led to an understanding of how nerves control muscles.

A.C./D.C – the Current Wars

The simple circuits we saw in subsection 5.2 use **direct current (d.c.)**. In d.c. circuits the current always flows in one direction from the positive side of the cell to the negative side. We can also use **alternating current (a.c.)**. This is where the current regularly reverses its direction, as the positive and negative sides of the circuit keep switching.

1 What is the difference between a.c. and d.c.?   [Total 2]

Figure 6.5 *A voltaic pile.*

Towards the end of the nineteenth century, companies and cities were just beginning to develop electricity supplies to homes and businesses. In the USA, this development caused a great debate over whether d.c. or a.c. should be used. The inventor and engineer Thomas Edison (1847–1931) wanted to transmit mains electricity using d.c. However, there was strong competition from the Westinghouse company, who wanted to use a.c. as suggested by Nikola Tesla, a Serbian physicist.

There are advantages and disadvantages to using each type of current. The main difference at that time was the efficiency of transmitting current. D.c. cannot have its voltage changed using a transformer. This causes d.c. to lose power over a short distance, and so the user needs to be within about 2 km of the power station. However, there is a small increased danger of electrocution from using a.c. When installed and used correctly, both a.c and d.c. are very safe. The financial advantages of large power stations which can serve a large area meant that d.c. would struggle to compete against the Westinghouse system and a.c. was eventually decided upon.

Edison had staked so much of his reputation (and quite a lot of money) on using d.c. that he could not let it fail. He ran a publicity campaign against a.c., highlighting its dangers. Edison's assistant Harold Brown (1869–1932) carried out many a.c. electrocution experiments on animals and together they made many political speeches falsely emphasising the number of people killed by a.c. Edison was the money behind the development of the a.c. electric chair for criminal executions, and he even tried to encourage people to use the word 'Westinghoused' to mean suffering death by electrocution. The public fear campaign failed, and the successful use of a.c. for the Niagara Falls hydroelectric power scheme was the turning point after which d.c. for transmitting electricity slowly died out. In fact Edison did buy into an a.c. company, but he stubbornly refused to use its technologies.

Figure 6.6 *a) Thomas Edison pushed for d.c. electricity supplies.*
b) Nikola Tesla showed how efficient a.c. could be.

?

2 Why did Edison go to such lengths to smear a.c. systems, when they are more useful and efficient for domestic electricity supplies than his d.c. system? *[Total 3]*

?

3 If you were Edison or Westinghouse trying to convince a council to invest in electrification for their town, give four reasons why the population would benefit from it.   *[Total 4]*

Many cities had invested heavily in d.c. to supply homes with electricity, so it was a long time before these were all replaced with more efficient a.c. – they are not easily compatible, so the same wiring cannot simply be switched. It was as late as 2007 that the final 60 d.c. customers in New York City were switched over to a.c.

The electric chair

The electric chair was a product of the Current Wars in the USA, but was never quickly effective or very humane. The electric chair, operating by sending a.c. through the brain, is supposed to kill its victim very quickly, using about 2000 volts and 7–12 amps. However, the different body sizes of the criminals it is used on means that executioners have never managed to determine the perfect combination of voltage, current and time to use.

Electricity and the body

Electricity can be used in several ways in people. In some people the nerve impulses which tell their heart muscles to contract do not reach all the heart muscles properly. The heart does not beat correctly. A pacemaker can be fitted under the skin and a wire goes into the heart. The pacemaker delivers minute shocks, or impulses, when needed, to the heart muscles. This regulates an abnormal heartbeat.

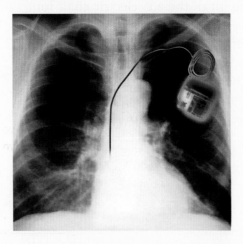

Figure 6.7 *The pacemaker shown on this X-ray delivers minute electric impulses to the heart muscles.*

If a person's heart has stopped beating or is beating very irregularly, an electric shock can be given, by a trained person, across the chest area. The shock stimulates the heart muscles to get them beating again. This is called defibrillation.

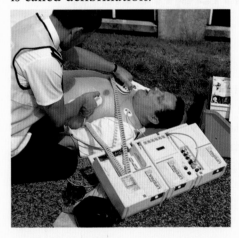

Figure 6.8 *A person having their heart restarted by defibrillation.*

When people tell lies, they very often sweat very slightly. As this makes the skin wetter than it would be normally, the resistance of the skin changes. Lie detectors work by measuring these changes in the resistance of the skin. However, lie detectors are not very reliable.

4 Why do you think lie detectors are unreliable?
[Total 1]

Questions

1 a) What was Galvani's theory of electricity? *[1]*

b) What was Volta's theory of electricity? *[1]*

c) Explain why they were both partly right. *[3]*
[Total 5]

2 Why might it be very dangerous to deliver an electric shock across the heart of a healthy person? *[Total 2]*

3 George Westinghouse was opposed to the development of the electric chair, and paid a very expensive lawyer to appeal against its use in the first case where a criminal was sentenced to execution by electrocution.
a) Why do you think he opposed it? *[3]*
b) Why do you think its use has now been stopped in virtually every country? *[2]*
[Total 5]

4 We use a great deal of electricity now. Before scientists discovered electricity, life would have been very different. Write a newspaper article describing what life would be like without electricity. *[Total 6]*

Modern and miniature electricity and magnetism

The age of electronics

The first electronic device was the **diode valve** built by John Fleming (1849–1945) in 1900, using a simple light bulb. A short while later Lee de Forest (1873–1961) invented the triode valve. These two components helped to start off the radio and television industry and were used in the first electronic computers in the 1930s and 1940s. Valves were large, expensive and used a lot of electric power. Modern microelectronics depend on tiny chips of silicon with complicated circuits on them.

The first silicon or **semiconductor** device was the **transistor**, designed in 1947 by William Shockley (1910–1989), John Bardeen (1908–1991) and Walter Brattain (1902–1987), who all worked at the Bell Telephone Laboratory in the USA. They won the Nobel Prize for their work in 1956. Another Nobel Prize was won in 2000 by Jack Kilby (1923–2005) for the invention of the integrated circuit – the microchip that is found in all computers, calculators, and most other electrical equipment. Kilby worked for Texas Instruments between 1958 and 1970. Robert Noyce (1927–1990) designed a similar device at the same time and set up a company known as Intel. As Noyce had died by 2000, only Kilby was awarded the Nobel Prize.

?

1 Name five electronic devices. *[Total 5]*

2 Why is it that most modern inventions are produced by people working in companies, rather than inventing on their own? *[Total 1]*

!

Noyce's company, Intel, is one of the biggest manufacturers of computer chips in the world, with about 80% of the microprocessor market in 2008.

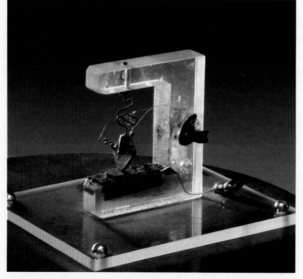

Figure 6.9 *A model of the first transistor invented at Bell Laboratories. The big model was used at a press conference to show how it works.*

The transistor pictured in Figure 6.9 is a large size model the inventors used to explain how transistors work. Their first working **prototypes** were about the size of a pea, but over the years transistors have been reduced in size so that now it is possible to connect millions of transistors in a space the size of a pinhead. This is why small devices like mobile phones can be so powerful in the functions they can carry out.

Nanotechnology

The trend to reducing the size of machines is happening across all areas of technology. LEDs used as everyday light sources are becoming very common, but these are almost out of date already, as molecule-sized light sources known as **quantum dots** are now available in many colours.

Electric motors need an electric current flowing in a coil in a magnetic field in order to turn. This idea was reduced to the micro-scale by a team of scientists at the University of California at Berkeley who produced a fully functional electric motor just 100 millionths of a metre across. However, they were not content with making a motor just the width of a human hair, and in 2003 unveiled the '**nanomotor**' which is less than half a **micrometre** wide.

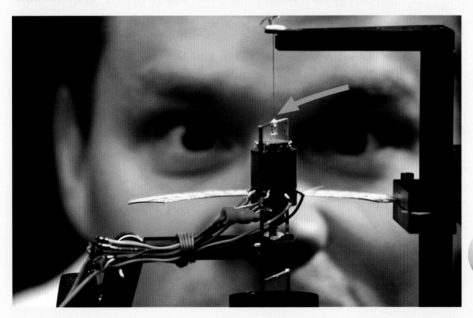

Figure 6.10 *Testing a micromotor. The motor is located inside the supporting cylinder (arrowed), and is about the same thickness as the supporting wire seen above it.*

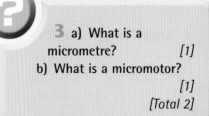

3 a) What is a micrometre? [1]
b) What is a micromotor? [1]
[Total 2]

Magnetic resonance imaging (MRI)

Sometimes doctors need to look at the soft tissues inside the body such as the heart or brain. X-rays are not suitable for this, as although bones show up very strongly on X-rays they tend to obscure the tissues behind them. MRI allows the organs inside the chest and head to be seen in much greater detail, without the bones showing as strongly, and without exposing the body to X-rays.

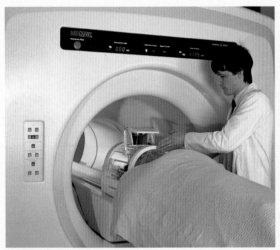

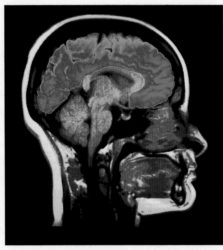

Figure 6.11 *This person is having an MRI scan. The results of the scan are shown on the screen.*

Three-dimensional images of the organs are generated using a magnetic field which is 1000 times stronger than the Earth's magnetic field. The nuclei (centre) of hydrogen atoms inside the body cells line up in one direction because of the strong magnetic field. As they realign weak radio signals are sent out. These signals are used to produce an image on a screen. As bone does not contain as many hydrogen atoms as soft tissue does, it does not show up as well and the soft tissue can be seen clearly. MRI can reveal if there is anything wrong in the organs, as diseased or abnormal tissue has a different appearance from normal tissue. For example, a tumour will show up as well as damaged tissue after a stroke.

?

4 How are MRI scans useful for doctors?

[Total 3]

Questions

1 Why are scientists and engineers always trying to reduce the size of the machines they have developed? *[Total 2]*

2 Suggest a practical use for a micromotor. *[Total 1]*

3 Suggest a practical use for a quantum dot. *[Total 1]*

4 a) What are the advantages of MRI over X-rays? *[2]*

b) What parts of the body do not show up well on an MRI scan? *[1]*

[Total 3]

End of section questions

1 Name all the lettered components in the circuit shown in Figure 1. *[Total 6]*

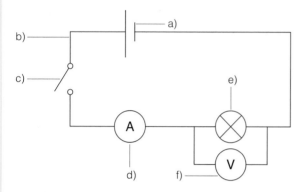

Figure 1

2 Charged plastic and charged glass will repel each other.
  a) What does that tell you about the charge on each? *[1]*
  b) If the plastic is put near some small pieces of paper what will happen? *[1]*
  c) What will happen if the glass replaces the plastic? *[2]*
  [Total 4]

3 A person shuffles around on a plastic stool and becomes negatively charged.
  a) Explain how the person becomes charged up. *[2]*
  b) What will happen to the charge when the person stands on the floor? *[2]*
  [Total 4]

4 Look at the circuit diagram shown in Figure 2.
  a) Which bulbs will light when switch 1 is closed? *[1]*
  b) Which switches need to be closed for all the bulbs to work? *[1]*
  c) One bulb needs two switches to be closed before it will work. Which one? *[2]*
  d) Redraw the circuit so that each bulb can be switched on its own. *[2]*
  [Total 6]

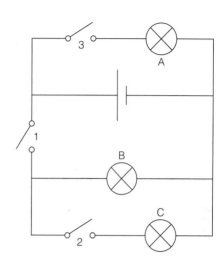

Figure 2

5 Some small pieces of steel have become mixed up in a box of copper rivets.
  a) How could you separate the pieces out using a magnet? *[2]*
  b) Would this work if there were aluminium pieces in the box of rivets? *[1]*
  [Total 3]

6 Why is iron used to make the core of an electromagnet? *[Total 2]*

7 The junior school has 10 magnets, which have been very roughly treated. The teacher says that the magnets are now very weak.
  a) Give a reason why these magnets could have lost their magnetism. *[2]*
  b) To help the school you offer to re-magnetise the magnets. How would you do this? *[2]*
  [Total 4]

8 A farmer wants to spray his field with pesticide. The droplets of liquid have a positive charge when sprayed.

   a) What are the advantages of this? [2]

   b) If the droplets were given a negative charge what difference, if any, would be noticed? [1]

   [Total 3]

9 Hassan wants the heater in his rabbit's hutch to work when it is cold and dark. Draw a circuit which will do this for him. [Total 2]

10 The local junior school is going to do some work on electricity. They need a safety leaflet that all the children can understand. Some of the younger children cannot read very well. Design a leaflet or poster to help the junior school. [Total 4]

11 Look at the circuit shown in Figure 3.

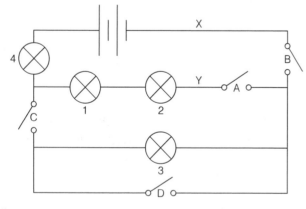

Figure 3

   a) What meter is placed at X to measure the current? [1]

   b) Which switches would you close for bulbs 1 and 2 to work? [1]

   c) How could you get bulbs 3 and 4 to light? [1]

   d) How could you get them all to work? [1]

   e) What would happen if just switch D were closed? [1]

   f) What would happen if switch B and D were closed? [1]

   g) A wire is placed between X and Y. What would happen now? [1]

   h) The wire is replaced with string. What would you expect to see? [1]

   i) If switches A, B and C are closed which bulb would be the brightest? [1]

   [Total 9]

12 P Design a burglar alarm using a relay.

13 P Find out three ways to make an electromagnet stronger.

14 P Find out how the thickness, length and material that a wire is made of changes its resistance.

15 R When an aeroplane is refuelled from a tanker the two machines are connected together with a conducting cable before the fuel is sent through a pipe. Why is this done?

16 R Magnetic levitation trains use electromagnets for movement. They can reach very fast speeds. Find out how they work.

17 R Michael Faraday invented the first transformer. Transformers are used in many places now. The charging unit for a mobile phone is a transformer. What job does a transformer do and where else might you find them?

What are investigations?

A **hypothesis** is an idea about how something works. It can be used to make a **prediction**. The purpose of an **investigation** is to test a prediction and find the answer to a scientific question.

> You might wonder what affects the pressure in a fluid. If you were a scientist, you would think up a hypothesis such as 'the density of the fluid affects the pressure'. You would use this hypothesis to make a prediction such as 'the denser the fluid, the higher the pressure', and then design a set of experiments to test the prediction by measuring the pressure in fluids of different densities.

The **data** produced in an investigation can be used to show whether the hypothesis is correct or not. If the data from several investigations support a hypothesis, the hypothesis becomes a **theory**.

New ideas are being suggested and tested in science all the time. Eventually, if an idea is well tested it may be accepted by all scientists. However, even well tested and established ideas can sometimes be proved wrong by further experiments or new ideas.

Many questions can be answered by doing experiments. These involve changing something and measuring the effects of changing it, such as in the example above. However there are other scientific questions that cannot be answered in this way. These questions may involve surveys, or careful observations, without changing anything.

> Scientists have answered many questions about why stars shine and how stars change as they get older. They cannot experiment on stars, but they have made many different observations of thousands of stars, and used all this information to develop ideas. They use these ideas to make predictions about what they will find if they study more stars. The predictions are tested by making further observations.

Scientists do not always have to carry out the investigations or observations themselves. A scientist with a new idea about stars could look at observations that have already been made to see if they fit with the idea. Observations made and reported by someone else are called **secondary sources**.

Variables and values

A **variable** is a factor than can change. Each variable can be described in words or numbers (with units), which are called **values**. Variables can be of different types:

- A **continuous variable** is something that can be one of a continuous range of values, and can have any numerical value.

- A **categoric variable** is described in words, or in numbers that cannot be split into smaller values.

> The length of a piece of wire is a continuous variable, but the material a wire is made from is a categoric variable.
>
> Shoe size is also a categoric variable as, although a shoe size is described using a number, it can only be 1, 1½, 2, etc, and never 1.1 or 1.7.

In most investigations you will choose a variable to change. This is called the **independent variable**. It is independent because its values don't depend on carrying out the investigation.

The **dependent variable** is what changes when the values of the independent variable are altered. This variable *depends* on the independent variable.

Investigations involve finding out whether there are **relationships** between different variables.

Fair testing

In most investigations there will be more than one variable that could be an independent variable. Since you only want to measure the effect of one independent variable, you need to stop all these other variables from changing. You need to try to control them. These are the control variables. Some control variables are very difficult to control.

> You are finding out if the length of a piece of wire affects its resistance:
> - the independent variable is the length of the wire (and is a continuous variable)
> - the dependent variable is the resistance (this is also a continuous variable)
> - the control variables are the material the wire is made from (a categoric variable), the diameter of the wire, and its temperature (both continuous variables).

Gathering data

The data you gather during an investigation needs to be valid, accurate and reliable.

- **Valid** data is data that is directly relevant to your investigation.

- **Accurate** data is data that is very close to the true value. You need to think about how accurate your data needs to be when choosing the measuring instruments for your investigation. When you choose a measuring device for measuring something you need to think about the **sensitivity** of the device. Instruments that are more sensitive will allow you to take readings with more significant figures which should therefore be more accurate. However, very sensitive instruments are not always needed

- **Reliable** data is data that will be the same if the experiment is repeated, or if someone else does the same experiment. You can make your results more reliable by taking each measurement several times and working out a mean or average value.

> A stopwatch will measure how long something takes to the nearest half second and is fine for school athletics. If you use a computer to do the timing, you may get a time to 1/100th of a second. The data will be much more sensitive if you use the computer and this is needed at the Olympics.

Presenting your results

The values of all variables should be recorded in a table, including the values of the control variables. If there is a relationship between the dependent and the independent variables in an investigation, there will be a pattern in the results. This is easiest to see by plotting a chart or graph. The independent variable is usually plotted on the horizontal axis. Draw a line graph if your independent variable is a continuous variable. Draw a bar chart if your independent variable is categoric.

If there is a relationship between the two variables, the points on the graph will form a line or a curve. Draw a line of best fit (or curve of best fit) through your points. The line or curve of best fit is the line you would get if all your measurements were perfectly accurate.

If you have gathered data using a datalogger and computer, you can use a spreadsheet program to produce graphs of your results.

The example investigation on the following pages shows you how to plan, carry out and report a typical investigation.

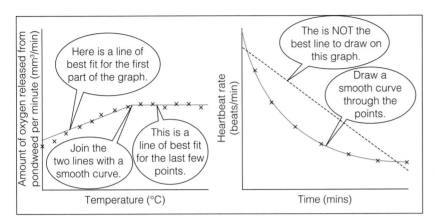

Figure 1.1 *Not all graphs form a straight line*

An example investigation

Consider an investigation into what affects how fast an object falls through wallpaper paste.

Plan

1 Think about what you are investigating. Describe briefly what you are trying to find out. This is your aim.

I want to investigate what affects the speed of an object falling through a fluid. Things fall very fast through air and water, and it would be difficult to measure their speeds accurately, so I will use wallpaper paste as my fluid.

2 Think of all the variables that could affect the thing you are measuring (the dependent variable).

Dependent variable = speed of object
The speed of the object could depend on:
- *the mass of the object*
- *the volume of the object*
- *the shape of the object*
- *the concentration of the wallpaper paste*
- *the temperature of the wallpaper paste*
- *the diameter of the tube.*

3 Choose one variable to investigate – this is the independent variable.

I shall investigate how the mass of the object affects the speed at which it falls through the wallpaper paste.
Independent variable = mass of the object.

4 Make a prediction about what will happen to the dependent variable as you change the independent variable. Try to explain why you made your prediction using scientific ideas.

I predict that as the mass of the object increases, its speed through the wallpaper paste will also increase. Twice the mass will go twice as fast. This is because there will be a larger downward force from a larger mass. The volume or shape has not changed and therefore the drag should be the same for each mass. The larger downward force will make the object move faster.

5 Plan how to carry out the investigation. Make it as accurate as possible. Include a list of the apparatus you will use, and explain how you will use it. Include a diagram if you can.

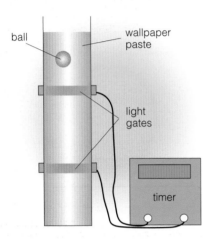

Figure 2

I will use:
- a tall, wide tube full of wallpaper paste, or a narrow tank
- balls of different materials, all the same size
- light-gates and a datalogger
- digital top-pan balance

To change the mass, I will use balls made from different materials. Each ball will be allowed to fall through the wallpaper paste. The speed will be measured using light gates and an electronic timer.

I will measure the mass of each ball using a digital top-pan balance.

To measure the speed I will use two light gates placed 30 cm apart. They will be connected to an electronic timer that automatically calculates the speed for me.

For each experiment I will hold the ball just under the surface and carefully position it over the light gates before releasing it.

I will use balls with masses of 50g, 60g, 70g, 80g and 90g.

6 Describe how you will make it a fair test.

To make my investigation a fair test I will keep the following variables (the control variables) the same for each test:
- the volume of the object
- the shape of the object
- the concentration of the wallpaper paste
- the temperature of the wallpaper paste
- the diameter of the tube containing the wallpaper paste.

7 Describe how you will make your results accurate, precise and reliable.

I will make my results accurate and precise by using a digital top pan balance for checking the masses of the balls.

I will make my results reliable by dropping each ball three times, and working out the mean time for each ball to fall through the light gates.

8 Describe how you will make it safe.

I will wear eye protection and not drop the ball into the wallpaper paste so that the paste does not splash over the bench. I will clear up any spills straight away in case anyone slips.

9 Show your plan to your teacher.

Obtain evidence

10 Do the experiment.

11 Record the results in a table. Always show all your repeated results, as well as the mean value. The independent variable goes in the left hand column, with the values for the dependent variables on the right. Make sure you include units for all your values.

Diameter of balls = 4.6 cm
Diameter of tube = 10 cm

*This result was not included in the average because it does not fit in with the others.

Table 1

Mass of ball (g)	Speed (cm/s)			
	Experiment 1	Experiment 2	Experiment 3	Mean
50	2.32	2.03	2.10	2.15
60	2.80	4.9*	2.91	2.86
70	3.61	3.38	3.52	3.50
80	3.65	3.55	3.59	3.60
90	4.00	4.15	3.85	4.00

Analysis

12 Plot a graph of your results, and describe any pattern shown.

As the mass increases the speed of the ball also increases. It looks like there will come a point where increasing the mass will no longer increase the speed.

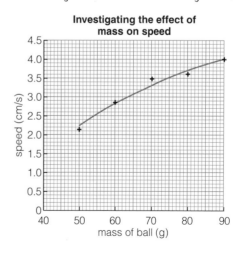

Figure 3

13 State the conclusion of the experiment and try to explain in scientific terms why this happened.

As the mass increased the speed of the ball increased. This agrees with my prediction except that doubling the mass does not double the speed. Although increasing the mass will increase the downward force.

Evaluation

14 Evaluate the investigation. This means that you should decide how good your experiment was, how reliable the results are and how you could improve it if you did it again.

My results look reliable because the points on the graph are all close to the line of best fit and they give a nice smooth curve. During experiment 2 for the 60 g ball, the result was higher than it should have been. I think this was because the bottom light gate was accidentally triggered before the ball got to it.

It was difficult to get the balls out of the tube after the first experiment and we lost some wallpaper paste for the second experiment. We would have liked some larger masses but we did not have any that were the same size.

The results seem to be good enough to come to a conclusion. The graph shows a clear pattern in the results and all the results are quite close to the line.

Rather than using a tube it would be better to use a large glass tank. This would make it much easier to get the balls out after each test. If it was long but not very wide, I could still use the light gates to measure the speed.

I would also be able to use larger balls, which might help me get a wider range of masses and a better graph.

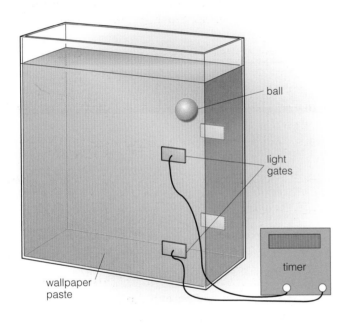

ball

light gates

timer

wallpaper paste

Figure 4

Glossary

absorb To soak up something.

accelerate To speed up or slow down.

acceleration The change in speed each second.

accurate A measurement that is accurate is one that is close to the true value.

air resistance Frictional force created by air passing over a moving object.

alternating current (a.c.) An electric current in a circuit which keeps changing direction, as in modern mains electricity supplies.

ammeter An instrument for measuring electric current.

amplitude The height of a wave or the depth of a trough.

AND gate A gate where two inputs must work to give one output.

angle of incidence The angle the incident ray makes with the normal.

angle of reflection The angle the reflected ray makes with the normal.

anticlockwise moment A moment that is tending to turn an object in an anticlockwise direction.

anvil A small bone in the inner ear.

artificial satellite A man-made object placed in orbit around the Earth.

asteroid A small lump of rock orbiting the Sun.

asteroid belt Collection of rocks orbiting the Sun between Mars and Jupiter.

atmospheric pressure The pressure exerted by the Earth's atmosphere.

attract To be pulled towards another object.

average speed Calculated from total distance travelled ÷ time taken for an object that may not be travelling at a steady speed.

balanced forces When two forces are the same strength but working in opposite directions.

big bang The beginning of the universe, when it started to expand from a tiny mass.

biogas Gas produced by rotting animal or plant matter that can be burnt.

biomass Any fuel that comes from plants, animals or their waste.

black hole The remains of massive star at the end of its life.

braking distance The distance a car travels while the brakes are trying to stop it.

categoric variable A variable that has a set of fixed values. These are usually words (e.g. blue green, orange) but can be numbers that only have a fixed set of values (e.g. shoe sizes).

chain reaction A series of nuclear transformations started by a single nuclear fission.

chemical energy Energy stored in the chemical bonds of a substance.

circuit An arrangement of electrical components.

clockwise moment A moment that is tending to turn an object in a clockwise direction.

cochlea coiled tube in the inner ear containing fluid and sensitive hairs to detect sound vibrations.

comet Ball of ice and dust moving in a large elliptical orbit around the Sun and going out past the planets.

compression Molecules moving closer together in a sound wave.

concave curved shape bending inwards like a cave.

conductor (electrical) Something which allows electricity to pass through it easily.

conductor (thermal) A material that allows thermal energy to flow through it easily.

controlled variable A variable kept constant during an experiment.

continuous variable A variable that can have any numerical value. Human height is a continuous variable.

convection A way that heat travels through liquids and gases.

convection current The flow of a liquid or gas created by one region being heated more than another.

conventional current The way current flow is described in textbooks, from + to –.

convex curved shape bulging outwards like the surface of a balloon.

crest The high part of a wave.

critical angle angle between a ray and the surface of a medium at which there is a change from refraction to total internal reflection.

data A collection of measurements.

decibel (dB) The unit for measuring sound levels.

density Mass per unit volume. Measured in kg/m^3 or g/cm^3.

dense Density is the mass of a certain volume of something. A dense material has a high mass for a given volume.

dependent variable The variable that you measure in an investigation. For example, you might measure the current in a circuit when you change the voltage. The current is the dependent variable.

diffuse reflection reflection from a rough surface in which light bounces in all directions.

diode A component in an electric circuit which allows current to flow through it in one direction only.

diode valve earliest component which allowed current flow in one direction only.

direct current (d.c.) An electric current in a circuit powered by cells, which always flows in the same direction.

distance–time graph A graph showing distance against time. The slope of the line on the graph shows the speed.

domain A neutral group of atomic magnets.

drag Air resistance and water resistance are sometimes both called drag.

dwarf planet A body orbiting the Sun that is big enough to be spherical, but not big enough to have cleared other bits of rock from its orbit.

eardrum Thin membrane in the ear that picks up vibrations.

echo The reflection of sound waves.

echolocation Using echoes to find something.

efficiency A way of saying how much energy a machine wastes. A machine with high efficiency does not waste much energy.

effort The input force applied to a mechanical machine such as a lever.

elastic limit The greatest stretching force that can be put on something without permanently changing its shape.

elastic potential energy The potential energy of an object due to its stretched or squashed shape.

electrical energy Energy of moving electrical charges.

electromagnet Coil of wire carrying a current with an iron core.

electromagnetic spectrum Forms of energy travelling as transverse waves.

electromagnetic (EM) wave A type of wave consisting of oscillating electric and magnetic fields.

electron Negatively charged particle that orbits the nucleus in an atom.

electron flow The movement of electrons through a wire from the negative terminal to the positive terminal of a cell.

electrostatic precipitator A machine in industrial chimneys used to clean smoke by removing particles of soot and ash from it.

elliptical Shaped like a squashed circle.

endoscope An instrument for viewing inside the body.

energy The ability to do work.

energy flow diagram A flow diagram to show energy transfers.

energy transfer Process by which energy is converted from one form to another.

evaporation A liquid turning into a gas at its exposed surface.

extension The total increase in length of a stretched object.

fair test A scientific test where all variables except the input variable and the outcome variable are kept constant.

fission The splitting of a heavy nucleus of an atom into two or more fragments.

force multiplier A mechanical device that converts a small force into a larger force.

fossil fuel All fuels that were formed from the remains of dead plants and animals.

frequency The number of waves per second passing one point.

friction A force that tries to slow things down when two surfaces rub against each other.

galaxy Millions of stars grouped together.

gamma radiation Energy given out by radioactive materials. Gamma radiation is similar to light and infra-red radiation, but it carries a lot more energy.

gamma rays The highest frequency, shortest wavelength, highest energy part of the electromagnetic spectrum. Emitted from the nucleus of radioactive atoms.

geostationary orbit An orbital path above the Equator in which it takes 24 hours to complete one orbit. The object stays in the same position above the Earth's surface.

global warming The gradual increase in the Earth's temperature, thought to be due to increased levels of carbon dioxide and other greenhouse gases.

gravitational potential energy The kind of energy stored by anything that can fall to the ground.

gravity The effect of gravitational attraction between masses.

greenhouse effect Heat trapped in the atmosphere by gases such as carbon dioxide and methane.

greenhouse gas A gas, such as carbon dioxide or methane, that traps heat within the Earth's atmosphere and contributes to the greenhouse effect.

hammer A small bone in the inner ear.

heat capacity The quantity of heat required to raise the temperature of a body by one degree.

heat energy Another name for thermal energy.

hertz (Hz) The unit of frequency.

Hooke's law The law stating that when a material is stretched the extension is directly proportional to the stretching force.

hydraulic system A force multiplying system using the transfer of pressure through a liquid.

hydroelectric A hydroelectric power station generates electricity from falling water.

hypothesis An idea about why something happens but that does not have very much evidence to support it. If more evidence is found to support the hypothesis, it becomes a theory.

illuminated An object that can be seen because light is reflected from it.

image The picture produced in a mirror.

incident ray The ray of light which travels towards a surface from a light source.

independent variable The variable that you change in an investigation. For example, you might measure the current in a circuit when you change the voltage. The voltage is the independent variable.

induced charge Charge put onto an insulator by being near a charged object.

infra-red (IR) Heat radiation; EM waves with a frequency just lower than visible light.

inner ear most internal part of the ear, including the cochlea, semi-circular canals and nerves to the brain.

input variable The variable in an experiment that is changed to observe its effect on another variable.

insulator (electrical) Something which reduces the flow of electricity going through it.

insulator (thermal) A very poor thermal conductor.

internal energy Energy a substance has due to the movement of its molecules. Also called thermal energy.

investigation Trying to find the answer to a scientific question by making measurements and/or observations.

joule The metric unit of energy or work.

kinetic energy Energy due to movement.

laterally inverted Back to front.

LDR Light dependent resistor. Its resistance decreases when light shines on it.

leap day An extra day at the end of February every 4th year.

leap year A year with 366 days. There is one leap year every 4 years.

LED Light emitting diode.

lift The force produced by aircraft wings as they move through the air.

lubricant A substance used to reduce friction.

luminous An object which gives off its own light.

lunar eclipse An eclipse of the Moon, when the Moon goes into the shadows of the Earth.

magnet Made from steel with a north and south pole.

magnetic field Area of magnetism around a magnet.

mass   A measure of the amount of matter something is made of. Measured in grams (g) or kilograms (kg).

medium   A substance.

meteor   A rock entering the Earth's atmosphere.

meteorite   Meteor hitting the Earth.

meteoroid   A small piece of rock orbiting the Sun, much smaller than an asteroid.

meteor shower   Lots of meteors seen together over a few hours or days.

micrometre   A millionth of a metre.

micromotor   An electromagnetic machine so small that its size can be measured in micrometres.

microwaves   EM waves between IR and radio in the EM spectrum, used for cooking and communications.

middle ear   part of the ear from the eardrum, including the ossicles, up to the outer edge of the cochlea.

molecules   Two or more atoms joined together.

moment   The turning effect of a force. Equal to the force applied multiplied by its perpendicular distance from the pivot point.

MRI scan   (magnetic resonance imaging) A medical scan showing internal organs and soft tissues.

nanometre   A billionth of a metre.

nanomotor   An electromagnetic machine so small that its size can be measured in nanometres.

natural satellite   Something orbiting a planet that is not man-made, e.g. the Moon.

neutron   Particle with no charge found in the nucleus.

newton   The unit for measuring force, named after Sir Isaac Newton.

newton meter   A force meter.

noise   A sound which is unpleasant.

non-renewable energy resource   A source of energy that takes millions of years to form and therefore cannot be replaced when it runs out.

normal   imagined line at right angles to a surface or boundary.

nuclear fusion   Nuclei joining together in the Sun giving energy.

nucleus   central part of an atom, made of protons and neutrons only.

ohm (Ω)   The unit for resistance.

opaque   A substance which will not allow light to pass through it.

OR gate   A gate where one or the other input must work to give an output.

original length   The length of an object before it is stretched.

outcome variable   A variable that is observed to see how it is affected by changing the value of an input variable.

outer ear   part of the ear from the opening to the air in as far as the eardrum.

parallel circuit   Arrangements of components with separate branches in the circuit.

pascal   A unit of pressure named after the seventeenth century French mathematician and physicist, Blaise Pascal; 1 pascal = 1 N/m^2.

penumbra   The grey part of a shadow where some light falls.

periscope   The arrangement of two mirrors or prisms which allows you to see round corners.

photocell   A device that converts solar energy into electrical energy.

pivot   The turning point of an object or system.

planet   A large object orbiting a star. The Earth is a planet.

polar orbit   Orbit that passes over both the north pole and the south pole of the Earth.

potential energy   Energy due to position or shape – elastic or gravitational.

prediction   Saying what you think will happen in an investigation and why you think it will happen.

pressure   Force per unit area; measured in N/m^2.

prism   A triangular shaped piece of glass or plastic which refracts light.

proton   Positively charged article in an atom found in the nucleus.

quantum dot   also known as nanocrystals, a molecule sized organic LED.

radiation (thermal) The transfer of thermal energy by electromagnetic waves.

radio The longest waves in the EM spectrum.

radioactivity Particles or energy emitted when atoms change into different types of atom.

rarefaction Part of a sound wave when the molecules move apart.

rectilinear Straight lines.

rectilinear propagation travelling in straight lines.

reed switch Switch operated by a magnet.

reed relay remote switch which can control a circuit, operated magnetically by a separate circuit.

reflected ray The ray of light which leaves a surface.

refracted ray The ray of light which changes direction when entering a more or less optically dense substance.

refraction The name given to the ability of light to change its speed and direction when travelling into a more or less dense substance.

regular reflection reflection from a smooth surface in which light rays bounce in exactly the same pattern.

relationship A link between two variables. If there is a relationship between two variables, one will change when the other changes.

reliable A measurement or observation that is reliable is one that will be the same when it is repeated.

renewable energy resource A source of energy that is continually being replaced.

repel To be pushed away from another object.

resistance How difficult it is for current to flow through an electrical component.

Sankey diagram Diagram showing energy transfers that includes relative values.

satellite An object in space that orbits a planet.

secondary sources A source that contains information that other people have gathered and written about.

semiconductor material which conducts but not very well.

sensitivity The more sensitive a measuring instrument is the more accurately it can measure something. A balance that can measure down to 1 g is less sensitive than one that can measure down to 0.001 g.

series circuit Components arranged in one continuous loop.

shooting star Another name for a meteor.

short circuit An easy route for the current to flow.

solar eclipse An eclipse of the Sun, when the Moon casts a shadow on the Earth.

solar panel A device that converts solar energy into heat energy. Usually used to heat water.

solar system A star with planets and other objects orbiting it.

specific heat capacity The quantity of heat required to raise the temperature of one kilogram of a substance by one degree Celsius.

spectrum Light refracted into the seven colours of the rainbow.

speed The distance travelled in one unit of time.

speed–time graph A graph showing speed against time.

static electricity Electricity which does not move easily.

stirrup A small bone in the inner ear.

stopping distance The distance a car moves while it is stopping. The stopping distance is equal to the thinking distance plus the braking distance.

strain energy Another name for elastic potential energy.

sustainable Using resources in a way that can continue into the future (without using up a resource, and without damaging the environment).

terminal velocity The steady speed reached by an object moving through a fluid when the driving force is balanced by the drag.

theory An idea about why something happens that has lots of evidence from investigations to support it.

thermal A rising air current due to local heating of air.

thermal conduction   The flow of thermal energy through a material.

thermal energy   The energy a substance has due to the movement of its molecules. Commonly called heat energy.

thinking distance   The distance a car travels while the driver is deciding to press the brake pedal.

thrust   The driving force produced by an engine or rocket.

tidal energy   Energy due to the movement of water produced by the gravitational attraction of the Moon and Sun.

tidal-stream turbine   An underwater turbine that generates electricity from currents in the sea.

total internal reflection   The situation when light has nowhere to refract and so reflects.

transfer   When energy is moved from one place to another or changed from one form into another we say it is transferred.

transistor   An electronic switch, also capable of amplification, made from semiconductor materials, especially silicon.

translucent   The description of a substance which will let some light through.

transparent   The description of a substance which will let most light through.

transverse wave   a wave in which the vibrations are at right angles to the direction the wave moves.

trough   The low part of a sound wave.

ultrasound   A very high frequency sound wave.

ultra-violet (UV)   EM waves with a frequency just higher than visible light; responsible for most skin cancers

umbra   The blackest part of a shadow where no light falls.

Universe   All the galaxies and the space between them.

upthrust   Upward force on an object in a liquid or gas.

valid   Valid data is data that is directly relevant to the question that is being answered.

values   The numbers (or labels) that a variable can have.

variable   A factor that can change in an experiment.

variable resistor   A component able to alter its resistance to current.

vibrate   To move about a fixed position.

virtual   Something which only appears to exist.

visible light   EM waves which can be detected by the human eye with wavelengths ranging from 400 to 700 nanometres.

voltaic pile   early chemical cell developed by Allesandro Volta.

voltmeter   device for measuring potential difference.

wavelength   The distance on a wave between two crests or troughs.

weight   The amount of force with which gravity pulls on an object; measured in newtons (N).

white dwarf   A small star formed when stars like the Sun run out of nuclear fuel.

work   The transfer or energy from one form to another.

X-rays   High energy EM waves used in medical imaging and airport security.

Index

Index

Index

Published by Pearson Education Limited, a company incorporated in England and Wales, having its registered office at Edinburgh Gate, Harlow, Essex, CM20 2JE. Registered company number: 872828

First published 2002
12
16

British Library Cataloguing in Publication Data
A catalogue record for this book is available from the British Library

ISBN 978-1-4082-3109-8

Design and illustration by HL Studios, Oxford
Picture research by Charlotte Lippmann
Printed in Malaysia (CTP-PPSB)

Acknowledgements

The author and publisher would like to thank the following individuals and organisations for permission to reproduce photographs:

(Key: b-bottom; c-centre; l-left; r-right; t-top)

3 POD - Pearson Online Database: Jules Selmes (b). 4 POD - Pearson Online Database: Gareth Boden (t). 5 iStockphoto: Markus Divis (b). 8 Pearson Education Ltd: Trevor Clifford (t). 9 Robert Harding World Imagery: (b). 12 Greg Evans International: (b). iStockphoto: Andrzej Burak (t). 14 Imagestate Media: (t). 15 POD - Pearson Online Database: Digital Vision. 16 Penny Johnson. 19 Science Photo Library Ltd: Martin Bond. 21 Robert Harding World Imagery: (tl). Science Photo Library Ltd: Martin Bond (tr). 22 www. tidalstream.co.uk. 23 Science Photo Library Ltd: Bernhard Edmaier. 29 FLPA Images of Nature: Nick Spurling (tl). TopFoto: (tr). 30 Science Photo Library Ltd: Physics Today Collection / American Institute of Physics (t); Radiation Protection Division / Health Protection Agency (b). 31 Science Photo Library Ltd: Centre Jean Perrin, ISM (l); Garry Watson (r). 35 iStockphoto: Chuck Babbitt; dejan suc (tr). 41 Science Photo Library Ltd: Adam Hart-Davis. 42 Science Photo Library Ltd: Alfred Pasieka. 55 Science Photo Library Ltd. 56 Getty Images: Popperfoto. 57 Science Photo Library Ltd: Cordelia Molloy. 58 Alamy Images: Nordicphotos/ Richard Kail (bl). Nature Picture Library: Adrian Davies (bc) (br). 59 Science Photo Library Ltd: Gustoimages. 60 NASA: Goddard Sapce Flight Center (bl); Jet Propulsion Laboratory (t) (bc). 61 Science Photo Library Ltd: NRAO/AUI/NSF. 64 Science Photo Library Ltd: Jerry Schad (b); Mehau Kulyk (t). 66 NASA: (t) (b). 67 NASA: (c). 68 NASA: JPL (bl). POD - Pearson Online Database: Photodisc/ StockTrek (t) (c). 69 NASA. 71 Science Photo Library Ltd: David Parker. 75 Science Photo Library Ltd: Dr Fred Espenak. 76 Science Photo Library Ltd: George East. 76 Science Photo Library Ltd: Professor Jay Pasachoff. 79 Science Photo Library Ltd: NASA. 84 Wellcome Library, London. 85 NASA: ESA and P. Kalas (University of California, Berkeley, USA) (b). Science Photo Library Ltd: (t). 86 Science Photo Library Ltd: Ria Novosti. 87 Science Photo Library Ltd: NASA (b); Planet Observer (t). 90 Getty Images: Claus Andersen. 96 Greg Evans International. 98 iStockphoto: technotr. 100 POD - Pearson Online Database: Photodisc/Bruno Herdt. 101 TopFoto: PA. 111 iStockphoto: Oleg Filipchuk. 116 TopFoto: Fastfoto Picture Library. 117 Science Photo Library Ltd: TRL Ltd.. 119 Art Directors and TRIP photo Library. 121 Art Directors and TRIP photo Library. 127 Science Photo Library Ltd: Martyn F. Chillmaid. 128 Reuters: Ethan Miller. 130 Pearson Education Ltd: Trevor Clifford. 132 Pearson Education Ltd: Trevor Clifford. 135 Pearson Education Ltd: Trevor Clifford (t) (b). 136 Pearson Education Ltd: Trevor Clifford (t) (r) (b). 138 Mark Levesley. 142 Science Photo Library Ltd: Martyn F. Chillmaid. 146 Science Photo Library Ltd: Andrew Lambert Photography. 148 iStockphoto: Richard Stanley (t). Science Photo Library Ltd: David Taylor (b). 149 Science Photo Library Ltd: Maximilian Stock Ltd. (b). 150 Science & Society Picture Library: Science Museum. 151 Science Photo Library Ltd: Library of Congress (t); Photo Researchers (b). 152 Science Photo Library Ltd. 153 Science Photo Library Ltd: Adam Hart-Davis. 154 Science & Society Picture Library: Science Museum. 155 Science Photo Library Ltd: Peter Menzel. 156 Science Photo Library Ltd: Scott Camazine (r); Simon Fraser/ Dept. Neuroradiology, Newcastle General Hospital (l)

Cover images: Front: POD – Pearson Online Database: Photodisc/Photolink/R. Morley

All other images © Pearson Education

Every effort has been made to trace the copyright holders and we apologise in advance for any unintentional omissions. We would be pleased to insert the appropriate acknowledgement in any subsequent edition of this publication.